J. M. BARRIE

LEONEE ORMOND

SCOTTISH ACADEMIC PRESS

EDINBURGH

Published by
Scottish Academic Press Ltd.
33 Montgomery Street, Edinburgh EH7 5JX

First Published 1987
SBN 7073 0504 7

British Library Cataloguing in Publication Data
Ormond, Leonee
  J. M. Barrie.—(Scottish writers).
  1. Barrie, J. M.—Biography   2. Authors, Scottish—19th
century—Biography   3. Authors, Scottish—20th century—
Biography
  I. Title   II. Series
  822′.8   PR4076

  ISBN 0-7073-0504-7

Printed in Great Britain by
Bell and Bain Ltd., Glasgow

SCOTTISH WRITERS

Editor
DAVID DAICHES

ACKNOWLEDGEMENT

The Scottish Academic Press acknowledges the financial assistance of the Scottish Arts Council in the publication of this volume.

CONTENTS

Preface   vii

I   Biography   1

II   Journalism and Criticism   11

III   The First Fiction   22

IV   The Early Plays   39

V   *Sentimental Tommy*   55

VI   *Tommy and Grizel*   72

VII   Barrie and the Theatre: 1902–1917   85

         The Admirable Crichton   90

         Peter Pan   100

         What Every Woman Knows   110

         1908–1917   115

VIII   *Dear Brutus* and *Mary Rose*   119

IX   *Farewell, Miss Julie Logan*   137

X   *The Boy David*   145

XI   Barrie and the Critics   149

         Bibliography   153

PREFACE

Today, half a century after his death, J. M. Barrie should be emerging from that trough into which popular authors invariably sink after death. Few, it is true, have fallen farther than Barrie. Once spoken of in the same breath as his friend, George Bernard Shaw, Barrie's work later became an object of derision and even opprobrium. Those terrible words, 'fey' and 'whimsy', words which Barrie himself came to hate, have served to condemn him to the outer darkness for years past. His plays, with the exception of *Peter Pan*, have been rarely performed, and his fiction has almost sunk out of sight.

The present volume sets out to put the case for Barrie as an original and unjustly neglected writer. It is important to stress the word 'writer'. If Barrie is remembered at all today, it is as an object of biographical curiosity. For Barrie to re-emerge as a writer worthy of general critical interest, it is essential that his achievement be judged in a literary context. His work has its roots in his own experience, but it is important to see it as more than thinly disguised autobiography. For this reason, I have refrained, as far as possible, from relying on biographical analysis. In the hands of others, this method has shed much light, but it is surely time for a new approach. If Barrie drew his inspiration from a private world, he was compelled, like any other author, to find a literary mode with which to express himself.

Barrie was a prolific writer. I have tried to sketch in the broad outlines of his career, but have chosen to concentrate on certain works, which have seemed to me to be representative and of high quality.

I am particularly grateful to the Director, Ralph W. Franklin, and to the staff of the Beinecke Library of Yale University. My period of research there was made possible by a Beinecke Library Fellowship. I owe a special debt to Marjorie Wynne, Research Librarian at the Beinecke Library, who did so much to make my visit to Yale memorable and happy. Among the others who made that visit possible, I should like to thank Professor Morton Cohen, Professor Louis Martz, Professor Janet Bately, Larry and Rose Hughes, Duncan Robinson and May Woods.

In the course of my work, a number of others have given me valuable help, among them Nicola Beauman, Olga Bennell, Andrew Birkin, Warwick Gould, Professor Gordon Haight, Dr. John Harvey, Dr. R. D. S. Jack, Dr. D. S. Mack, Pat Nightingale, A. V. B. Norman, Jane Soutar, Angus Wrenn and Professor Katharine Worth.

I acknowledge with thanks those who have given me permission to quote from manuscript sources: the J. M. Barrie Estate and Mr. and Mrs. William Bell.

My husband, Richard, has been, as ever, the most valued of critics and supporters. My whole family, including my sons, Augustus and Marcus, have accompanied me, with varying degrees of enthusiasm, to performances of Barrie's plays. I am grateful for their comments and their company.

L.O.

ABBREVIATIONS

ALI	*Auld Licht Idylls*
CP	*The Definitive Edition of the Plays*, ed. A. E. Wilson, 1942
GH	*The Greenwood Hat*, 1937 (privately printed 1930)
JL	*Farewell, Miss Julie Logan*
L	*Letters*, ed. V. Meynell, 1942
LWB	*The Little White Bird*
LM	*The Little Minister*
MLN	*My Lady Nicotine*, 1890
MO	*Margaret Ogilvy*, 1896
S	*McConnachie and JMB, Speeches by Barrie*, 1938
ST	*Sentimental Tommy*
TG	*Tommy and Grizel*
WAMS	*When A Man's Single*
WT	*A Window in Thrums*

All references to Barrie's prose works in the text are either to the Uniform Edition, or, where a date is given above, to the first edition. Plays are dated from the first performance.

CHAPTER 1

BIOGRAPHY

James Matthew Barrie was born at Kirriemuir in Forfarshire on 9 May 1860, the third son and seventh surviving child of David Barrie and of his wife, born Margaret Ogilvy. Kirriemuir, the Thrums of James Barrie's early writing, depended on two industries; weaving and stone quarrying. Barrie was connected with both. His father was a hand-loom weaver and his mother's father, Alexander Ogilvy, had worked as a stone mason in the quarries on the edge of the town.

Kirriemuir stands among beautiful country. A few miles down the road to the South is Glamis Castle, which must have fuelled James Barrie's interest in Shakespeare's *Macbeth*. To the north of the town, lie the lovely valley of Glen Clova (probably Barrie's Glen Quarity) and Cortachy Castle.

James Barrie's birthplace, now a museum, is in the row of low-built houses then known as The Tenements. During his childhood, his father's loom occupied one of the small rooms downstairs, while the other held the prepared cloth. There were box beds for children in this second room, but otherwise, the whole family lived and slept in the two rooms above. Later, when David Barrie joined a communal work-shed behind the house, the family spread downstairs.

Hand-loom weaving was a declining industry and David Barrie took a post in the accounts office of a linen factory in Forfar in 1871. A year later he was back, with a better job in a linen factory in Kirriemuir. The Barrie's new house, 'Strathview' in Southmuir was larger, though at first they shared it with their mother's brother.

The catastrophe of James Barrie's childhood has been described many times. Early in 1867, when James was six, the Barries' second son, David, then nearly fourteen, was killed in a skating accident. The mother never recovered from the loss of her favourite child, and James describes in *Margaret Ogilvy* how he set out to take David's place, and to comfort his mother. From this circumstance, it is claimed, came Barrie's mother fixation, that central pillar of so much Barrie criticism. Barrie was, of course, devoted to his mother, and even went to the lengths of publishing a biography of her, *Margaret Ogilvy*, in 1896. What strikes the reader of *Margaret Ogilvy*, however, is not so much hagiography as ventriloquism. Like his own *Sentimental Tommy*, Barrie displays a remarkable gift for playing a role, for entering into another person's consciousness. Once mastered, this same gift lay behind his great powers as a dramatist.

The death of his brother had a second, and in many ways more profound, effect upon the young Barrie. It taught him that human life is precarious, and happiness uncertain. The lesson was underlined by the sudden death of his sister's fiancé in 1892. As he grew older, he drew the conclusion that those who die young have preserved something that survivors inevitably lose. This theme runs through Barrie's mature work far more insistently than the relationship of mother and son. His final play, written after many years of silence, was, tellingly, entitled *The Boy David*.

The eldest Barrie son, Alick, became a schoolteacher, and later an inspector of schools. In 1868, James went to live with him in Glasgow, where the boy attended the Glasgow Academy. When Alick left Glasgow in 1871, James went home to Forfar, and to school at the Forfar Academy. The following year he was back in

Kirriemuir, before returning to live with Alick in Dumfries. Between 1873 and 1878, James Barrie had his longest spell at a single school, at Dumfries Academy. From there he went on to Edinburgh University, without a scholarship, and without great distinction.

The years at University, from which he graduated in 1882 with an M.A., did not excite him. The dreary lecture notes which survive provide at least one explanation for his boredom. Only David Masson, Professor of Rhetoric and English Literature, managed to capture his imagination. Masson apart, only the Edinburgh theatre and some part-time reviewing provided Barrie with intellectual stimulation.

In January 1883, Barrie began a two year stint as a journalist, writing special articles for the *Nottingham Journal*, before the proprietors decided that they could do without him, and he lost his job. Returning to Kirriemuir, he fired off a series of articles to editors in London. A few were accepted by Frederick Greenwood of the *St. James's Gazette*, and, with this encouragement, Barrie turned south in March 1885. Living simply in London, he completed hundreds of articles and stories, a fair proportion of which were selected for publication.

During these 'grub-street' years, Barrie wrote a number of plays, two of which, *Ibsen's Ghost* (1891) and *Walker, London* (1892), were successfully produced by John Lawrence Toole, a famous comic actor and theatre manager. Fiction, however, loomed larger in Barrie's ambitions. In 1888, he began the series of books on humble Scottish life, centred on Thrums (Kirriemuir), with which he made his name: *Auld Licht Idylls* (1888), *A Window in Thrums* (1889), and the more fantastical *The Little Minister* (1891).

From these early days, Barrie's chief working-tool was a series of note books, thirty-nine of which are now housed in the Beinecke Library at Yale University. In these tiny books Barrie jotted down ideas for his work, often listing six or seven hundred ideas in a single note book. Some can be recognised as germs and then revisions of plans for plays and novels. Others remain as unused ideas. Single lines, sudden flashes of inspiration, are intermingled with highly developed plots. The most startling revelation in the notebooks is that Barrie had almost no new ideas after the early 1900s. At the time when he was planning his successful early plays, *The Admirable Crichton* (1902) and *What Every Woman Knows* (1908), he was already making notes for *Dear Brutus* (1917), *Mary Rose* (1920) and *Shall We Join the Ladies?* (1921).

In 1894, Barrie married a young actress, Mary Ansell. It has been said that the marriage was not consummated. Though this seems unlikely, it is certain that Barrie was a less than eager lover, and never satisfied his wife's strong sexual instincts.

Barrie's notebooks dating from the years immediately before his marriage to Mary Ansell are full of revealing autobiographical notes. Preliminary ideas for *Sentimental Tommy* merge into diary entries documenting a sexual power struggle between an unnamed man and an actress with the initials M.A. The male protagonist is said to have been shy at college, to have missed the 'flirting days'. Now, able to diagnose the behaviour of women, he uses this knowledge to gain a hold over them.

> This sentimentalist wants to make girl love him,
> bullies & orders her (this does it) yet doesn't
> want to marry — The first love affair wd have
> effect of no longer making him wish to marry (or
> even in first he may not have wanted to do so).

> Such a man, if an author, wd be studying his love
> affair for book. Even while proposing, the thought
> of how it wd *read* wd go thro' him.

First, her independence, 2nd hates herself at feeling it go, 3rd proud to be his slave — Their talk of this — his pride in making her say she is his slave & he her master — Her wistful humbleness about future.

They arrange to love, not to marry.[1]

It is dangerous to regard anything Barrie wrote as a clue to his real nature. He remained detached and watchful even as he wrote these private notes. Seen in the context of many other statements about his fear of marriage as a trap or a prison, they do indicate the causes of his wife's unhappiness. All the evidence points to the fact that her husband neglected her. Mary Barrie was a gifted designer, both of gardens and interiors, and the couple's homes were her creations rather than her husband's. She set the style, organised their social life, but, in the end, the loneliness was more than she could bear.

When Mary left Barrie in 1909, it was with a younger writer, Gilbert Cannan, one of Barrie's associates in the campaign for the reform of theatre censorship. Mary Barrie's second marriage proved more disastrous than her first. She never had the children she longed for, and Cannan was eventually engulfed by insanity. In her desperate desire to find a new life, Mary had forced Cannan into a marriage which severely increased the strains upon him. Barrie remained loyal to his former wife, never blamed her for her desertion, and later insisted upon paying her an allowance.

The problems of Barrie's relationship with Mary find their clearest expression in *Sentimental Tommy* (1896) and its sequel, *Tommy and Grizel* (1900). These books represent Barrie's most determined bid for immortality as a writer, and it is strangely appropriate that the hero, Thomas Sandys, is, like himself, an artist who uses those about him as raw material for his work.

Once the trauma of the divorce was past, Barrie settled back thankfully into bachelor life. He moved into a flat in Adelphi Terrace, overlooking the Thames. Here, and in a second flat two floors above, he remained for the rest of his life. Bernard Shaw and Harley Granville Barker and his wife, the actress, Lillah McCarthy, lived nearby. This was the period of Barrie's closest association with his fellow dramatists. The censorship agitation of 1907–9, in which he played a leading part, had little impact save in the founding of the Dramatists' Club, of which Barrie was a member. In 1910, Barrie was involved in a pioneering repertory season at The Duke of York's Theatre, with Shaw, Galsworthy and Granville Barker. Some of the most radical modern plays of the period were performed, including Barrie's short feminist masterpiece, *The Twelve Pound Look*. With Shaw and Pinero, Barrie was an active member of the management committee of the Royal Academy of Dramatic Art. His one-act play, *Shall We Join the Ladies?* launched their new theatre in 1921 with a cast of stars.

The 1910 repertory season, a highly experimental venture, only took place because of Barrie's close association with the American impresario, Charles Frohman. Frohman backed the season financially because of his boundless confidence in Barrie. Until Frohman's death on the *Lusitania* in 1915, Barrie, certain of his support, could do more or less as he liked in the theatre. Frohman took over the management of the Duke of York's Theatre in 1897, and ran what was once described as an old fashioned stock company there, with Dion (Dot) Boucicault as his director, and with Gerald Du Maurier, Irene Vanbrugh and Harry Irving as his chief performers.

Irene Vanbrugh probably worked as closely with Barrie as any actress. She starred in *Ibsen's Ghost* and

Walker, London, was the original Lady Mary in *The Admirable Crichton* (1902) and Amy in *Alice Sit-By-The-Fire* (1905). *Rosalind* (1912) was written for her, and her last Barrie role was Miss Isit in *Shall We Join the Ladies?*.

Mrs. Patrick Campbell, Ellen Terry, Fay Compton, Ellaline Terriss, Nina Boucicault, Hilda Trevelyan, Lillah McCarthy and the American actress, Maude Adams, were among those who starred in Barrie's plays. Unfailingly kind, he sent them letters full of delightful compliments and lavish appreciations. Similar letters were despatched to beautiful women like Millicent, Duchess of Sutherland, who received them in the spirit in which they were sent. The embarrassing exception was Florence Hardy, who misinterpreted Barrie's intentions, and arrived in London on Thomas Hardy's death, expecting a proposal of marriage.

The proof of Charles Frohman's nose for theatrical success was his decision to put on Barrie's children's play, *Peter Pan*, following its rejection by Beerbohm Tree. The play was first performed in 1904 and became an annual ritual in London and New York as well as a huge commercial success. Changes in the copyright laws, and a flourishing theatre in both Britain and America brought Barrie some of the highest rewards ever earned by a dramatist. His generosity was proverbial, and he dedicated the royalties from *Peter Pan* to the Hospital for Sick Children in Great Ormond Street.

The genesis of Peter Pan lies in the games which Barrie played with the sons of Arthur and Sylvia Llewelyn Davies, whom he met around 1897. Their mother was a daughter of the writer and cartoonist, George Du Maurier, and a sister of the actor, Gerald. Strongly attracted to her both as a beautiful woman and an exemplary mother, Barrie lavished gifts and affection upon her and her family. When Arthur

Llewelyn Davies died in his forties from cancer in 1907, Barrie more or less took over support for the widow and children, eventually sending four of the five boys to Eton. After Sylvia's tragic death in 1910, from the same disease, Barrie informed her sons that she had accepted his proposal of marriage.

The five orphan boys gave Barrie the family he had longed for, but, even here, tragedy struck. The two to whom he was closest both died young, George, the eldest, in the first world war, and Michael, the fourth, in a drowning accident at Oxford in 1921. There are grounds for believing that he commited suicide.

Barrie's wealth and wit made him a favourite with high society, the epitome of what a famous establishment author should be. He was one of the best-known and best-loved authors of his age. In his later years, he employed Lady Cynthia Asquith, a daughter of Lord Wemyss, as his secretary, and acquired through her and her sons a second surrogate family. Persistent allegations that Cynthia Asquith, like Sylvia Llewelyn Davies, exploited Barrie for his wealth, much of which Cynthia Asquith inherited, may or may not be true. Barrie was an astute man with few illusions about human nature, and he may have accepted the happiness which both women brought him, without questioning their motives too closely.

Barrie received his share of worldly honours. He became a baronet in 1913 and received the Order of Merit in 1922. He was Rector of St. Andrews University, and Chancellor of his own University.

In the second half of his working life there were long periods when Barrie felt that he had nothing worthwhile to say. With his gift for catching the public mood, he made a few excursions into writing film-scripts, among them adaptations (apparently never produced) of *As You Like It* and *The Taming of the Shrew*. More successful was *The Real Thing At Last*, a silent film parody of *Macbeth*, performed as part of the war effort in 1916. Barrie wrote prolifically, turning out one-act plays and burlesques, many in aid of good causes, but had little faith in his own ideas. After *Dear Brutus* (1917) and *Mary Rose* (1920) Barrie almost abandoned writing. A letter to the American actress, Maude Adams, describes the loss of buoyancy and inspiration which prevented him from working on a promised play:

> That love story! Well I still hope to get at it, but the days pass, the weeks, the months, and I am in a sort of dead-alive condition.... Perhaps I am word played-out. Awell a day! But I have had these horrible spells before now, and hope to get past this one. I think the chief thing against me is that I seem to have ceased to believe in my knowledge of human nature. I find people so different from what I had thought them that it brings me to the ground. I am too lonely (I wrote the word as if it were 'lively'). Oh that it were![2]

Among the few things which did appear in Barrie's last years was a short masterpiece in prose, *Farewell, Miss Julie Logan*, which was circulated with *The Times* at Christmas 1931. Then, in 1934, Barrie met his last actress, the Austrian exile, Elizabeth Bergner. As so often before, he offered to write something for her. Reviving an old idea, he suggested a play about Mary Queen of Scots. The actress declared that she wanted to play the young King David.

Barrie believed *The Boy David* to be his finest work, and he became increasingly desperate to see it in production. First the actress was promised elsewhere, and then she became seriously ill. When the play finally opened in Edinburgh on 21 November 1936, Barrie himself was too ill to attend his only Scottish first night. The comparative failure of *The Boy David*, which ran for fifty-five performances in London, deepened the gloom of Barrie's last days. He died on 19 June 1937, at the age of seventy-seven.

NOTES

1. Beinecke Library, Barrie Mss, A2/12.
2. Letter of 2 May 1919, Beinecke Library, Barrie Mss, A3.

CHAPTER II

JOURNALISM AND CRITICISM

A reader of Barrie's early books would conclude that
literature was frowned upon in Kirriemuir. 'The
ministers in the town did not hold with literature'
(ALI, 219), we are told in *Auld Licht Idylls*, and Miss
Ailie, the school-teacher in *Sentimental Tommy*, wrestles
with feelings of guilt whenever she takes a romance out
of the lending library. Shakespeare's corrupting plays
are buried in the back garden, and the minister's wife
and children have to read *Waverley* and *Ivanhoe* in secret.
'Mr. Dishart,' 'did not approve of story-books' (ST,
230). In James Barrie's own home, however, no such
edicts were applied. His mother was a great reader,
Carlyle, Gibbon, George Eliot and Margaret Oliphant
being her particular favourites. The Barries themselves
owned few books, the Bible and *Pilgrim's Progress* among
them, but others were borrowed from the circulating
library at 'a penny for three days' (MO, 46), and
James subscribed to a children's magazine called
Sunshine. *Robinson Crusoe* was the first library book
borrowed for James, who was to be addicted to stories
about islands for the rest of his life. 'Many writers of
romances have had romantic notions' he wrote later,
'but you can't do better than wreck your hero on an
island. To this day I would not pass a book by in
which there was a desert island'.[1] In his Dumfries days,
he discovered R. M. Ballantyne's *Coral Island*, which he
far preferred to *The Swiss Family Robinson*, and Rider
Haggard's *King Solomon's Mines*. He went on to discover

Jules Verne's *The Mysterious Island* and the novels of
Captain Marryat and of Fenimore Cooper.

As a boy, Barrie shared his mother's passion for the
works of Thomas Carlyle, and he used to look out for
Carlyle himself during his school-days in Dumfries. In
later life he acknowledged that the flame had soon
burnt out. His admiration for Walter Scott, however,
lasted all his life. He told and retold the stories of
Ivanhoe and *Kenilworth* to his friends at Forfar Academy,
and both novels are deeply woven into the imaginative
life of *Sentimental Tommy*. Barrie had read all Scott's
novels by an early age. In an essay of 1891, he tried
to select the best, but concluded that *A Legend of
Montrose* apart, all were structurally flawed. Jeanie
Deans was top of the poll of heroines, and Hal o' the
Wynd, in *The Fair Maid of Perth*, of heroes. Edinburgh
brought out Scott's finest descriptive powers, especially
the passages in *Guy Mannering*.

A large element in Barrie's admiration for Scott was
the fact that he wrote about specifically Scottish
subjects. Barrie felt a similar loyalty to Margaret
Oliphant, about whom he drafted a number of articles,
and for whose *A Widow's Tale and other Stories* he wrote
an introduction in 1898. The enthusiasm was mutual,
for Mrs. Oliphant was one of the the critics to greet
Auld Licht Idylls with applause.

With the work of English Victorian writers Barrie
acquired an early familiarity. He deeply admired
Thackeray, and references to Becky Sharp are scattered
through his notebooks and essays. He adapted the last
chapters of *Vanity Fair* for one of his first plays. Like
most contemporary opinion, he preferred the early,
more humorous novels of Dickens, *Pickwick Papers*, and
the theatre scenes from *Nicholas Nickleby*, to the later
ones. Barrie's most Dickensian passages of writing occur
in the opening chapters of *Sentimental Tommy*, where
Tommy is living in the London slums. Both writers

share a powerful concern with children and their welfare, but Barrie once launched a scathing attack on Dickens for introducing 'children into his stories that he may kill them to slow music'.[2]

In 1890, Barrie planned a story about a man who falls in love with Emily Brontë after reading *Wuthering Heights*. He travels to Haworth, only to arrive for the funeral. To Barrie, Emily Brontë, by no means a well-known writer at the time, was 'our greatest woman' (S, 159). Reading her sister's *Shirley* in 1918, he rated Charlotte far below her. George Eliot was another well-thumbed author from Kirriemuir days. A comment in a notebook of 1888 is exceptionally acute: 'George Eliot polishing at phrases kept reader back — phrases like stones to climb over in way — stop to pick them up'.[3] In the following year, Barrie judged *Silas Marner* a 'great novel', but inferior to the work of Thomas Hardy, who had 'enriched the fiction which deals with heaths and villages much more than George Eliot'.[4] Both writers were to have a considerable influence on him when he came to write fiction himself.

In the late 1880s and early 1890s, Barrie contributed a series of critical essays to the *Contemporary Review*, on Meredith, Hardy, Sabine Baring Gould and Kipling. Each reveals a knowledge of the whole range of work of the novelist under discussion. Barrie was keenly aware of the distinction between popular fiction and serious literature: 'The majority read novels not to think, but to keep themselves from thinking',[5] and 'It is the law of the land that novels should be an easy gallop',[6] he says in his 'George Meredith' essay of 1888. Meredith, Barrie considers, makes his readers 'pant uphill'.[6] Writing about Rudyard Kipling in 1891, Barrie puts the point again: 'The best of our fiction is by novelists who allow that it is as good as they can give, and the worst by novelists who maintain that they could do much better if the public would let them'.[7]

Among living authors, the young Barrie most admired
Meredith and Hardy. By the 1890s, he had become a
trusted friend of both; Meredith was thirty-two years
his senior and Hardy twenty. Both in notebook entries
and a series of articles on Meredith, Barrie tried to
identify the essence of his quality. He accused Meredith
of avoiding the commonplace and so allowing humour
to be 'swallowed by wit, greater by lesser'.[8] For Barrie,
Meredith's work had 'no heart',[8] was obscure,
undramatic and full of improbable dialogue. But, if he
sometimes 'misses,' he often 'rings the bell'.[9] Most
novelists of the time were 'mere petty twaddlers'[10]
beside Meredith. He excelled in creating unforgettable
characters, and this, for Barrie, as for many critics of
his day, was the ultimate touchstone of excellence in a
writer of fiction.

Barrie had a fine ear for language and phraseology.
His work on Kipling's sentence structure is sharp and
penetrating. In the Meredith essay, unjustifiably
ignored in recent studies of Meredith criticism, Barrie
attempts to pinpoint the idiosyncracies of Meredith's
style. He notes that all the characters, regardless of age,
employ the same elaborations of speech. Everyone 'talks
Pilgrim's Scrip'.[11]

Barrie's own debt to Meredith is less one of style, in
spite of Meredithean passages in *Tommy and Grizel*, than
of subject-matter. The younger novelist's preoccupation
with the idea of the sentimentalist and the egoist owes a
good deal to Meredith. It is appropriate that, in 1910,
he should have arranged for the first production of
Meredith's fragment of a play, *The Sentimentalists*.

That Barrie was an advocate of 'showing' rather than
'telling' is evident from his essay on Hardy of 1889. 'No
living novelist keeps more in the background than Mr.
Thomas Hardy, who is, therefore, a storyteller.... We
do not want to hear the points of the horse, but to see
him running'.[12] Barrie regarded Hardy as the greatest

'realist' of his age, a chronicler of a dying world: 'Railways and machinery of various sorts create new trades and professions, and kill old ones...the shepherds and thatchers and farmers and villagers, who were, will soon be no more, and if their likeness is not taken now it will be lost for ever'.[13]

Barrie wrote this comment on Hardy in the year when his own *A Window in Thrums* was published, and it applies equally to his own early work. Reviewers of Barrie's fiction frequently compared him to Hardy, as well as to the early George Eliot, and to Oliver Goldsmith. Like these three writers, Barrie saw himself as a chronicler of a vanishing world, trying to steer between the Scylla and Charybdis which he believed Hardy had successfully negotiated; sentimentality and ugly naturalism: 'There are clever novelists in plenty to give us the sentimental aspect of country life, and others can show its crueller side. Some paint its sunsets, some never get beyond its pig-troughs or its ale-houses; many can be sarcastic about its dulness'.[13]

If Barrie admired the novelists of the older school, he was far less complimentary about those of his own generation, believing that the novel was under attack from various heresies. His fullest statement on the subject is an article of 1890 entitled 'Brought Back from Elysium', a late Victorian version of Swift's *Battle of the Books*. Five classic novelists: Fielding, Smollett, Scott, Dickens and Thackeray, are ranged against five newcomers: Realist, Stylist, American, Elsmerian and Romancist.

The force of Barrie's argument is, that in turning fiction into a 'fine art', the writers of the late nineteenth century had become obsessed with technique, and had impoverished the narrative tradition of the novel. As Thackeray tells the moderns in his closing riposte: 'perhaps if you thought and wrote less about your styles and methods and the aim of fiction, and, in short, forgot yourselves now and again in your stories, you might get on better with your work'.[14]

Sympathy was another quality which Barrie found wanting in the modern novel. He admired Kipling's sharpness and aggression, but found him cynical, a criticism which he also turned on Sabine Baring Gould: 'Sympathy is the ink in which all fiction should be written; indeed, we shall find, on examination, that the humour, which some say is the novelist's greatest gift, and the power of character-drawing by which others hold, are streams from this same source'.[15]

If, as seems likely, Barrie cherished an early ambition to become a novelist, he went through a long apprenticeship before his first novel was published in 1887. As a boy, he put more effort into his plays than his stories; and, as a young man, he first approached fiction through the medium of the short essay and sketch.

The reasons for his delayed career as a novelist were largely financial. When Barrie travelled south, he had to achieve independence at once. Endowed with boundless energy, he felt no inhibitions about turning his pen to an endless stream of articles, essays and stories on anything which caught his imagination, showing a remarkable resistance to the psychological effect of literary rejection. At the outset, particularly after moving to London in 1885, he took it for granted that a high proportion of his work would be refused and steadfastly continued to bombard editors with his pieces. With magazines catering for a voracious readership, it was inevitable that Barrie, who could tell an absorbing tale, would succeed.

His early periodical writing falls into three main groups. There are stories of humble Scottish life in Thrums; lighter sketches and humorous pieces; and finally literary criticism, the best concerned with fiction, but with an occasional glance at the London theatre.

Barrie wrote a long and comparatively scholarly essay on John Skelton and planned a series of papers on early satirists, which again suggests that he regarded periodical journalism as a temporary interlude before devoting himself to serious writing. Barrie's criticism reveals a keen mind, with a feeling for the quality of the writing before him, and an awareness of the important issues which needed to be faced.

In the sketches and stories, by contrast, Barrie's mind turned towards vivid narrative, often with a touch of drama, rather than towards theoretical exposition. In the best of his early journalism he draws the reader into a comfortable relationship with himself as narrator, assuming the role of a pipe-smoking, slightly bemused man, capable of witty and detached observation. Much of the humour of Barrie's short pieces lies . in his assumed air of self-deprecation.

It is hard to define their precise literary genre. Some are sketches, where Barrie emulates the example of Charles Lamb and other romantic essayists in employing a strongly personal tone. Like Lamb, whom Barrie greatly admired, he often seems to ramble as ideas strike him, never adopting the rational dialectical approach of the eighteenth-century essayists. Occasionally, a narrative thread, or even an historical one, runs through as a connecting link. Local Kirriemuir legend lies behind 'Byron at Glamis' or 'The Battle of Cabby Latch'. More often, the stimulus is something humorous rather than dramatic, which has recently happened to the author. He tells how, on a visit to Stratford-upon-Avon, he dropped his tobacco-pouch, and went back to look for it, or how a friend had given him a flower to look after, which had subsequently died.

A characteristic example is 'My First Cigar', which appeared in a collection of essays on smoking, *My Lady Nicotine* of 1890. The piece was prompted by memories of the birth of his niece, Lilian, eldest daughter of his brother, A. O. Barrie, in 1878. James Barrie, a schoolboy of eighteen, was living in his brother's house at Dumfries.

In six pages, Barrie sets out to evoke the tension between the narrator and his brother as they sit together by the study fire. Somewhat implausibly, we are asked to believe that the narrator has no foreknowledge of the birth. Irony is implicit in the way in which the older narrator tells the story through the innocent eyes of the boy. The younger brother notices that the elder one has something on his mind, because their regular ritual for avoiding one another seems to have broken down.

> As a rule, when we were left together, he yawned or drummed with his fingers on the arm of his chair to show that he did not feel uncomfortable, or I made a pretence of being at ease by playing with the dog or saying that the room was close. Then one of us would rise, remark that he had left his book in the dining-room, and go away to look for it, taking care not to come back till the other had gone. In this crafty way we helped each other. (MLN, 20)

This is a masterly account of the tacit understandings of family life. Under pressure, however, the established patterns of behaviour prove inadequate. On the evening of the birth, not even provocative political statements, nor a deliberate mistake about the Battle of Waterloo, can rouse the elder brother from his state of anxiety.

On closer analysis the guileless portrait of the elder brother turns out to be far from complimentary. We learn that he habitually scowls when credited with being the younger boy's father, that he is unable to carry on an argument: 'because he was disappointed if I was right and stormed if I was wrong' (MLN, 21).

Though the focus of the story might appear to be the elder brother, or even the birth upstairs, our attention remains fixed on the boy's problems in trying to find the appropriate role for himself. 'I don't think I ever liked my brother better than on that night; and I wanted him to understand that, whatever happened, it would make no difference between us' (MLN, 21). The boy becomes tired, and wants to go to bed: 'That however, would have been selfish; so we sat on defiantly' (MLN, 23).

After the birth, the boy fears that he may be asked to hold the baby, or 'that they might want to call it after me. These, of course, were selfish reflections; but my position was a trying one' (MLN, 23). The narrator wonders what he should say to his brother, but, when the latter descends he is shocked by his evident levity. Nothing is said for twenty minutes, until the elder brother finds a suitably indirect form of words: 'Well, young man, do you know that you are an uncle?', to which the boy eventually manages to get out a reply, '"Boy or girl?"' (MLN, 24). Then, as a comic assertion of adulthood, the boy takes his first cigar, a concession, perhaps, to the fact that this is a book of essays about smoking.

Certain characteristics mark this as a Barrie tale. Notes about a boy's fear of having to hold a baby, or of having it named after him, turn up in a number of Barrie's early notebooks, and this was evidently the germ of the story. The author manages to get inside a boy's mind, conveying both his embarrassment and his sense of inadequacy when faced with an adult crisis. Birth is always a problem for Barrie, and the traditional reticence between brothers provides no framework for any display of feeling: 'I could not jump up and wring his hand. I was an uncle' (MLN, 25), thinks the boy, reacting once again to his own position. The reversal of roles at the end of the story, when the solemn elder brother becomes flippant, only to be confronted by the portentous silence of the younger, completes the story's paradoxical shape.

Barrie's humour is rarely entirely relaxed. Discomfort and unease are the basis of his comedy. He perhaps comes nearest to straightforward humour in one of the best-known stories, 'My Brother Henry' and in the series of pieces about a nephew, Primus. Primus comes to stay, and then orders and re-orders his Christmas and birthday presents. The result is self-mockery at the author's expense:

> I think I'll have a book again but not a fairy tale or any of that sort, nor the 'Swiss Family Robinson', nor any of the old books. There is a rattling story called 'Kidnapped' by H. Rider Haggard, but it is only five shillings, so if you thought of it you could make up the six shillings by giving me a football belt. Last year you gave me 'The Formation of Character', and I read it with great mental improvement and all that, but this time I want a change. (MLN, 165)

'My Brother Henry' is a comic treatment of one of Barrie's favourite notions: that we owe our existence to those who believe in it. An entirely imaginary person, like the narrator's brother, Henry, begins to take on a whole range of attributes, from a difficult wife to two children who are drowned in the Firth of Forth. The story, first published in 1888, predates Oscar Wilde's *The Importance of Being Earnest*, where Jack Worthing also invents a brother. In both cases, the brother starts life as a way of getting out of difficulties, and ends by creating more problems than he solves. Barrie's narrator is hard put to it to satisfy the curiosity of his friend, Scudamour, whose original confusion over the narrator's own name led to the invention of Henry. Like Jack Worthing, the narrator eventually kills off his creation, and pretends to be mourning a non-existent relation.

As with 'My First Cigar', 'My Brother Henry' is an account of embarrassment. Within its tiny compass, it is gloriously funny, but the theme needs little adjustment to change its nature entirely. Henry, existing in a curious limbo of his own, is as 'real' as any character in literature. The difference lies only in the narrator's pointing out his lack of substance and telling us how the character acquired his skeletal role. In Barrie's mature writing, the 'might-have-beens', like Margaret in *Dear Brutus*, become projections of what we dream of, but can never have. By contrast, the unwanted Henry is thankfully returned to the world of the imagination from which he came.

NOTES

1. 'Boys' Books: Their Glorification,' *Two of Them* (New York, 1893), p. 199.
2. 'The Humour of Dickens', *An Auld Licht Manse* (New York, 1893), p. 219.
3. Beinecke Library, Barrie Mss, A2/9.
4. 'Thomas Hardy: The Historian of Wessex', *Contemporary Review* (July 1889), p. 60.
5. 'Mr. George Meredith's Novels', *Contemporary Review* (October 1888), p. 577.
6. Ditto, p. 575.
7. 'Mr. Kipling's Stories,' *Contemporary Review*, (March 1891), p. 364.
8. Beinecke Library, Barrie Mss, A2/9.
9. 'Mr. George Meredith's Novels', p. 576.
10. Beinecke Library, Barrie Mss, A2/9.
11. 'Mr. George Meredith's Novels', p. 578.
12. 'Thomas Hardy', p. 57.
13. Ditto, p. 59.
14. 'Brought Back from Elysium', *Contemporary Review* (June 1890), p. 854.
15. 'Mr. Baring-Gould's Novels', *Contemporary Review* (February 1890), p. 206.

CHAPTER III

THE FIRST FICTION

Barrie's early career parallels that of other nineteenth-century novelists. Charles Dickens began his writing life as a journalist, before combining a collection of his published pieces to create *Sketches by Boz*. Barrie was to do the same with *Auld Licht Idylls*. A closer parallel is provided by the French writer, Guy de Maupassant. Maupassant, dissatisfied with journalism and short-story writing, believed that he could only scale the literary heights by becoming a novelist. Like the young Barrie, he wrote his fiction in episodic form. The novels retain the overall shape of a series of short stories, run together to make up a linear narrative. In Barrie's case, this episodic shape never acquired the roundness and unity expected in novel writing of the post-James era. In contrast to Maupassant, he was frequently tempted to exchange the tight construction of his shorter writing for a more prolix and expansive style, writing in a mixture of genres within a loose framework.

One problem may have been the speed at which he wrote. *Better Dead*, *Auld Licht Idylls* and *When a Man's Single* all appeared within a year (November 1887–October 1888), *A Window in Thrums* followed in 1889, *My Lady Nicotine* (a book of essays and stories) in 1890, and *The Little Minister* in 1891. Not surprisingly, reviewers began to suggest that Barrie should take a rest, and give himself time to shape a serious work of literature.

The first and third of Barrie's full-length books are

both, in their different ways, attempts to jump on to popular bandwagons. *Better Dead* is a 'shilling shocker' or horror story, *When a Man's Single* a romantic novel.

It is hard to find many virtues in *Better Dead*, where the hero joins a society devoted to ridding the world of unnecessary people. The short story from which it derives, 'The Body in the Black Box', refused by the *Cornhill Magazine* and apparently never published, is altogether more chilling than the full-length novel. In the story, the unamed narrator describes how he watches his shadow in a shop window. Totally isolated, he finds that only his shadow will nod to him in greeting. When a young clerk mocks him, the narrator decides to kill him. For weeks he follows the clerk about, and when he finally commits the deed exchanges roles with the dead man. The narrator takes on his victim's job and marries his fianceé. He has found a place in society.

This is an early treatment of a theme often explored by Barrie in later works. He was certainly inspired by Gothic tales of the alter-ego or doppelgänger, but the question of identity is central to many of Barrie's stories and plays. The fear lest another should usurp one's being is closely related to his numerous discussions of role changing. When, in *Better Dead*, he shifts the idea out of the realms of the mind, it becomes less haunting and more contrived.

When a Man's Single has more individuality than *Better Dead*. Rob Angus, a Thrums saw-miller, becomes 'single' when the child he has adopted dies. He finds work as a journalist in Silchester (Nottingham), and eventually marries the upper-class heroine, Mary Abinger. The novel shows little of the penetration of the shorter pieces, but Barrie does attempt to express more intimate psychological truths than in *Better Dead*. He opens writing through the consciousness of a child, Davy, only to startle the reader by allowing her to die.

Several hostile reviewers criticized these Thrums passages. George Meredith saw it quite differently: 'you must pardon me for choosing in preference the first and last chapters — especially the first, which is to me comforting as a Scotch broth-pot at the bubble of a quiet stew. More than the too many cooks, the too strong a fire under a pot will spoil the nourishing broth'.[1]

Barrie's role playing theme is well expressed through the character of Mary Abinger's brother, Richard, a lawyer secretly working as a journalist. Abinger tries to explain to himself why he is so hesitant about marrying the girl who loves him:

> is it my fault that my passion burned itself out in one little crackle? With most men, if the books tell true, the first fire only goes out after the second is kindled, but I seem to have no more sticks to light.
>
> I am going to be married, though I would much rather remain single.... Is marriage a rash experiment when the woman loves the man for qualities he does not possess, and has not discovered in years of constant intercourse the little that is really lovable in him?
>
> Is a man necessarily a villain because love dies out of his heart.... [Nell] will have for a husband a man who is evidently incapable of a lasting affection for anybody. That, I suppose, means that I find myself the only really interesting person I know. (WAMS, 267–8)

Not smoothly handled perhaps, this extended monologue is far more entertaining than the main plot of the novel. Abinger's reference to books in which relationships take a certain path, and to life, where things seem very different, relates him to the deepest emotional preoccupations of Barrie's early writing. The notebooks are full of poignant passages about Barrie's fear of marriage, and the gulf between the reality of what he felt and the response expected of him.

The second book, *Auld Licht Idylls*, is a collection of sketches and stories, set in the Scottish town of Thrums. It was this random grouping of reprinted essays and stories, with no pretentions to being a novel, which set Barrie on the path to fame and success.

'An Auld Licht Community' was among the first of Barrie's articles to be accepted by Frederick Greenwood. It appeared in the *St. James's Gazette* of 17 November 1884, and was followed by several more of the same kind. These were later collected together and extended into *Auld Licht Idylls*. In his biography of his mother, *Margaret Ogilvy*, Barrie describes how he contrived to satisfy the demand: 'I thought I had exhausted the subject, but our editor wrote that he would like something more of the same, so I sent him a marriage, and he took it, and then I tried him with a funeral, and he took it, and really it began to look as if we had him' (MO, 64).

Regionalism was in the air, as Greenwood must have known well. Thomas Hardy had been writing about Wessex for more than a decade, and the Irish Dramatic Movement was just beginning. Barrie's writing, both here and in the other Thrums books, is characterized by a precision of local detail, bringing home to the reader the simple lives and often cramped conditions of the Scottish poor. Several reviewers compared him to painters of the Dutch and Flemish Schools, like Rembrandt and Teniers; another, seizing a contemporary comparison, described him as a photographer in print. While his subject was ostensibly the early years of the century, Barrie must, to some extent, have been drawing upon his own observations. The chapter called 'Cree Queery and Mysy Drolly' tells the story of a knife-grinder who takes to hand-loom weaving so that he can keep his much-loved mother at home. In the account of their single room, Barrie writes with an exactitude of observation which helps to dilute the excessive sentiment of the story itself:

> The flooring was only lumpy earth, with sacks spread over it to protect Mysy's feet. The room contained two dilapidated old coffin-beds, a dresser, a high-backed arm-chair, several three-legged stools, and two tables, of which one could be packed away beneath the other. In one corner stood the wheel at which Cree had to fill his own pirns. There was a plate-rack on one wall, and near the chimney-piece hung the wag-at-the-wall clock, the timepiece that was commonest in Thrums at that time, and that got this name because its exposed pendulum swung along the wall. The two windows in the room faced each other on opposite walls, and were so small that even a child might have stuck in trying to crawl through them. They opened on hinges, like a door. (ALI, 139–40)

Barrie's source for his account of the Auld Lichts was the stories told him by his mother, herself brought up as a member of this extreme branch of the Presbyterian Church. On her marriage, she had joined another break-away group, the South Free Congregation. Much has been made of the fact that Barrie himself had no direct knowledge of the Auld Licht faith, and George Blake, in his *Barrie and the Kailyard School*, finds the 'guying' of his fellow townsmen 'revolting' and 'disquieting'.[2]

The term Auld Licht arose in the mid-eighteenth century as a result of a series of splits and secessions in the Church of Scotland. At a later date, the expression was used generally to denote the Calvinist wing of the Presbyterian Church, with its stern discipline and hell-fire preaching. The Auld Lichts expected their ministers to give inspirational sermons, and detested any form of show in religious ceremonies. There was no music in their services and no decoration in their churches. The leading members of the community were antipathetical to secular books or culture of any kind.

In *The Little Minister*, the Auld Lichts take on the character of Orwellian thought police, persecuting anyone who steps out of line. Their intransigence helps to illuminate the dilemma of a provincial artist desperate to escape from the restriction of small town life. Like James Joyce, Barrie attempts to justify his flight from home on the grounds of the repressions of local society. At the same time, Barrie recognised in the Auld Lichts one of the pillars of that traditional way of life, already on the wane, which he chronicled with such feeling. Like George Eliot and Thomas Hardy, Barrie saw the destructive effect of mechanization and the spread of religious conflict. In the manner of Walter Scott, he sets the scene a few years before the present, but it is clear that his analysis is of contemporary society. Not only is he describing a church in decline, but a whole way of life belatedly disappearing in the wake of the industrial revolution.

A number of reviewers of *Auld Licht Idylls* and *A Window in Thrums* linked Barrie to a specifically Scottish school of writers. The obvious connection with Robert Louis Stevenson was made, much to Barrie's disgust. Reviewers also drew attention to Barrie's extensive use of Scots dialect words, complaining of their incomprehensibility. Barrie's notebooks show that he consciously collected Scots terms, probably from his mother, and that they did not form part of his natural vocabulary. The narrator glosses a number of these unfamiliar expressions, tacitly assuming that they will not be understood, but retaining them as a token of authenticity in the text. Barrie's great strength lies in his rendition of dialogue, and the introduction of Scots is an integral part of both his humour and his pathos.

A passage from *When a Man's Single* shows how the author adapts the spelling to convey the ring of the Thrums accent. Only the words 'speired' and 'kent' (asked and known) are likely to be unfamiliar to a southern readership, although, looked at as a whole, the passage may seem foreign:

> 'Ye was lang in gettin' a man yersel, Jinny', said Tammas to an elderly woman.
>
> 'Fower an' forty year', replied Jinny, 'It was like a stockin', lang i' the futin', but turned at last'.
>
> 'Lassies nooadays', said the old woman who smoked, 'is partikler by what they used to be. I mind when Jeames Gowrie speired me: "Ye wud raither hae Davit Curly, I ken", he says. "I dinna deny't", I says, for the thing was well kent, "but ye'll do vara weel, Jeames", says I, an' mairy him I did'.
>
> 'He was a harmless crittur, Jeames', said Haggart, 'but queer. Ay, he was full o' maggots'.
>
> 'Ay', said Jeames's widow 'but though it's no' for me to say't, he deid a deacon'. (WAMS, 22–3)

The effect of the use of dialect terms, and of phonetic spelling, is to establish the separate identity of Thrums as a particular Scottish town. In *Sentimental Tommy*, Barrie incorporates his dialect words into the structure of the novel, but he was not confident enough to do that in the 1880s. Here regional speech helps to define difference by standing out in marked contrast to the King's English of the educated narrator. The humour of the passage takes on a pithy quality which the dialect helps to accentuate. Barrie knew George Eliot's *Adam Bede* well, and he emulates one of Mrs. Poyser's aphorisms in Jinny's reference to her long wait for a proposal of marriage: 'like a stockin', lang i' the futin', but turned at last'.

The introduction of regional dialect, itself threatened

and disappearing, is a part of Barrie's picture of
change. The movement away from cottage industry is a
leitmotif throughout the Thrums series, right down to
the *Tommy* novels. The process of mechanization had
been slower in Scotland than in the English Midlands,
where it had been ably chronicled by George Eliot in
Silas Marner. Eliot could survey the textile industry
from outside, but Barrie's own family life had been
directly affected by it. In *Margaret Ogilvy*, Barrie
describes the transformation of Kirriemuir into a new
town: 'Before I reached my tenth year... Where had
been formerly but the click of the shuttle was soon the
roar of "power", handlooms were pushed into a corner
as a room is cleared for a dance' (MO, 20–1).

In the passage which follows, Barrie assesses the
effects of the change, balancing advantages and
disadvantages. On the credit side is the end of grinding
poverty, and of the physical disfigurement of the
weavers, no longer bent double over their hand-looms.
Against this, he sets the fact that only the young can
find work in the factories, and that the employment of
women had broken up the patterns of home life. Now
that boys of fourteen can find work: 'Not in batches are
boys now sent to college' (MO, 22).

The Thrums series is in some ways a lament for the
hand-loom weaver. Bent and worn, he retains moving
nobility and independence of his own. Hendry
McQumpha in *A Window in Thrums* works all his life for
little reward, supporting a crippled wife and a
daughter, with small contributions from a son working
in London. At the opening of the book, the narrator,
the dominie of Glen Quarity, Gavin Ogilvy, returns to
the McQumphas' deserted cottage, leading us into the
story through his recollection of the hard life once lived
there:

> Into this humble abode I would take any one
> who cares to accompany me. But you must not

> come in a contemptuous mood, thinking that the
> poor are but a stage removed from beasts of
> burden, as some cruel writers of these days say: nor
> will I have you turn over with your foot the
> shabby horse-hair chairs that Leeby kept so
> speckless, and Hendry weaved for years to buy,
> and Jess so loved to look upon. (WT, 1–2)

There is nothing escapist about this. The narrator's
position may introduce a patronizing note, but the
account of poverty is too concrete to be sentimental.
Only with the mention of the horse-hair chairs is an
obvious play made for the reader's feelings, and, even
here, the argument is a sound one, the plea for
understanding perfectly justified.

David Barrie, like most of his neighbours, was a
member of the Kirriemuir Chartist Association. In the
summer of 1839 calls for political reform provoked
reverberations throughout Scotland, and particularly
among textile workers who faced a large drop in
income. Drawing upon local memories, Barrie
introduces the Kirriemuir riot of 1839 into *The Little
Minister*. Here, as in all the early books, he makes clear
his sympathy for the hard-used weavers.

Barrie was not averse to delivering direct political
thoughts. In 1885, he wrote a Carlylean 'political tract
for the times', 'The Battle of Cabby Latch'. Here he
told the story of an earlier rising by starving weavers,
unable to pay for bread, and driven by hunger to
attack the local farmers. The substance of the essay was
later incorporated into *Auld Licht Idylls*. Barrie closes his
account of the rising with a warning to the government
that this is the inevitable result of desperation.

In describing the hardships of a declining
community, Barrie was careful to avoid the 'seamy'
style which he disliked so much in the naturalist
novelists. 'Happily, there is more of Teniers than of
Zola is his realism; more happily still, there is more of

Wilkie than of Teniers',[3] wrote the critic of *The Spectator*, commending Barrie for restricting himself to the pious poor.

On the other hand, Barrie by no means 'fudges' the issue of poverty. One of the best passages in *The Little Minister* is in Chapter 12, where the Doctor and the Minister go to remove an old woman, Nanny Webster, from her home in order to take her to the workhouse. Barrie's remarkable skill with stage dialogue is prefigured in the creation of the atmosphere between these three characters — their speech and their silences. The Doctor, embarrassed and kindly, attempts to convince himself and his companion that all is for the best. The Minister, Gavin Dishart, younger and more openly moved, 'dared not let himself speak' (LM, 101). It is the old woman who has to keep up the conversation and, retaining her self-possession, act as hostess. Her chief concern is that no-one should see her disgrace, and it is this which finally unhinges the Doctor. It is fitting, if overly dramatic, that a scene in which two professional men find themselves incapable of implementing the poor-law, should end with the advent of another woman, the half-gypsy, half-aristocrat, Babbie.

At least one reviewer took Barrie to task for inadequate realism in his treatment of humble Scottish life. The critic of *The Academy* noted that he had ducked the issue of alcoholism in *Auld Licht Idylls*.[4] During 1888 Barrie was wrestling with this very subject in his notes for *The Little Minister*: 'Man will break out in sweat with terror lest he yield to temptation & drink — on such men the smell of it terrible temptation — solitude or weariness of mind & body, or excitement engenders the craving'.[5]

In these first notes even the young Minister is tempted by an inherited craving for drink, the weakness which had rendered his own father an object of disgust to his mother, Margaret. In the end, the drinking of the father is only hinted at, and the Thrums drunkard is a relatively minor character. The change altered the whole tone of the novel.

If the idea of the hero's potential fascination with drink was rejected, Barrie continued to explore the theme of temptation. Gavin, he thought, might be tempted by adultery or bigamy with Babbie: 'Suppose just when G. to take a fatal step has some .proof of mother's love...is saved'.[6] The notion of a tragic ending for the novel, with Gavin stoned out of the town by his parishioners, was still in Barrie's mind as a possibility until a comparatively late stage. Like Meredith in *The Egoist*, however, he compromised by making Babbie a fiancée not a wife, and allowed his lovers to marry. Robert Louis Stevenson, who must have heard of Barrie's plans, wrote to remonstrate;

> *The Little Minister* ought to have ended badly; we all know it did; and we are infinitely grateful to you for the grace and good feeling with which you lied about it. If you had told the truth, I for one could never have forgiven you. As you had conceived and written the earlier parts, the truth about the end, though indisputably true to fact, would have been a lie, or what is worse, a discord in art. If you are going to make a book end badly, it must end badly from the beginning. Now your book began to end well. You let yourself fall. in love with, and fondle, and smile at your puppets. Once you had done that your honour was committed — at the cost of truth to life you were bound to save them.[7]

Having started out as a serious 'problem' novel, *The Little Minister* ended as a work of romantic fiction, its implausible love story contrasting oddly with the wry treatment of love and marriage found in the other

Thrums books. Barrie has little gift for describing a passionate relationship between a man and a woman, and he has to fall back upon the social division between the lovers to inject tension into their relationship. By contrast, *Auld Licht Idylls* and *A Window in Thrums* present a picture of the banal and very practical reasons for which men and women marry. If James, the errant son in *A Window in Thrums*, carries a lady's glove about with him, that is because he has been to London and taken to reading. In Thrums it is the young women who usually take the initiative and lead the young men to the altar. Marriage is less a question of love than a matter of sensible arrangement.

In the humorous 'Courting of T'nowhead's Bell' from *Auld Licht Idylls*, Bell will accept the first proposal she is made by either of her suitors, whether or not he is her favourite. So important is it to her to be married. Barrie explored the same idea in several subsequent works, including *The Professor's Love Story* (1894). In 'Lads and Lasses', another of the *Auld Licht* sketches, Barrie tells the story of Jamie Whamond, who, having married one daughter of a farmer instead of her sister, decides to make the best of it: '"I'm thinkin"', Jamie said at last, a little wistfully, "that I micht hae been as weel wi' Chirsty"' (ALI, 92).

This lack of romance might be read as a statement of class prejudice. The Minister can fall in love, but not the hand-loom weaver. It would be more accurate to see the distinction as a literary rather than a social one. Like Shaw, Barrie was well aware that women commonly take the lead in sexual relations, and that the 'happy marriage' ending of the English novel bore little relation to his experience of human beings. After the 1890s, no important play or novel by Barrie ends with the union of a young couple.

The picture of love and marriage in Thrums is, of course, deliberately exaggerated for comic effect. While this might be seen as another jibe at Kirriemuir's expense, in literary terms it represents the deliberate avoidance of naturalism. Not until *Sentimental Tommy* did Barrie describe the suppressed sexuality of the young farm-workers who lived for weeks on end 'huddled together...in squalid barns more like cattle than men and women' (ALI, 45). His account of their behaviour at the Muckley Friday Fair is dour, but far from unsympathetic. Early in the day, the narrator tells us, the men are bashful, but, as the dark falls, drunkenness removes their inhibitions:

> The Jeans were as boisterous as the Jocks, giving them leer for leer, running from them with a giggle, waiting to be caught and rudely kissed. Grand, patient, long-suffering fellows these men were, up at five, summer and winter, foddering their horses, maybe, hours before there would be food for themselves, miserably paid, housed like cattle, and when the rheumatism seized them, liable to be flung aside like a broken graip. As hard was the life of the women: coarse food, chaff beds, damp clothes their portion; their sweethearts in the service of masters who were reluctant to fee a married man. Is it to be wondered that these lads who could be faithful unto death drank soddenly on their one free day, that these girls, starved of opportunities for womanliness, of which they could make as much as the finest lady, sometimes woke after a Muckley to wish that they might wake no more? (ST, 204–5)

This is Barrie at his best as a regional novelist. Forty years before, in her essay on the German social historian, Riehl, George Eliot had reminded her readers that farm labourers were not idealized figures of pastoral landscape art, but often coarse and insensitive. Barrie's description of the Muckley Fair is far more direct and explicit than anything written either by George Eliot or by Barrie's hero, Thomas Hardy.

In realist fiction, the narrator generally provides the consensus, the single vision which lends an apparent actuality to the whole. Where the narrator is given a strong fictional presence, is 'dramatized', voyeurism is a lurking danger, and it is a danger to which Barrie regularly succumbs. The problem of creating an illusion of reality without the reader being conscious of the narrator's presence is one to which the greatest novelists have addressed themselves. Barrie's vivid pictorial style in these early books very often accentuates the intrusive presence of the narrator.

In *Auld Licht Idylls*, Ogilvy the dominie provides a loose link between a group of sketches which vary considerably in style and approach. Ogilvy's is the eye which ranges over the whole town and district, sometimes describing the scene, sometimes relating stories and anecdotes. In the more coherent, though still loosely constructed, *A Window in Thrums*, Ogilvy is a summer visitor to the house of a poor weaver and his family. So aware do we become of the cramped cottage in which the story is centred, that our sense of the narrator's presence becomes almost physical. Ogilvy lives above the family in a tiny garret room, from which he descends to survey the life below.

In the final chapters of *A Window in Thrums*, Barrie describes the effect on the family of the ruin of the son. If there seems to be a debt to Wordsworth's 'Michael', it is perhaps less a matter of literary influence than of shared background. The exile of the son is, in any case, a recurrent theme in Scottish literature. Jamie McQumpha has gone to London and became a barber, but he returns every summer. As he bids them goodbye for ever, his parents and sister are unaware of the fact. The narrator's retrospective knowledge lends a special poignance to an already emotional episode. He invites the reader to frame the room with him, and to look at the picture: 'You must walk softly now if you would cross that humble threshold. I stop at the door. Then, as now, I was a lonely man, and when the last night came the attic was the place for me' (WT, 193). The reader's instinct is to see a picture of mother, father and two children, gathered together for the last time. The presence of the narrator disturbs the scene: 'We went upon our knees', says Ogilvy, including himself. In the last sentence, the reader is reminded to step back with the narrator and observe: 'By its meagre light [the lamp's] you may take the final glance at the little family; you will never see them together again' (WT, 202).

While Ogilvy's role as narrator in *The Little Minister* becomes more clearly defined, his position as an outsider is correspondingly intensified. Now we learn that he had once been bigamously married to Margaret Dishart, by whom he had a son, Gavin. Ogilvy has been long since parted from them. When Gavin comes to Thrums as the new Minister, Ogilvy does not disclose his identity. His determination never to be seen again by Margaret effectively removes him from the centre of the action: 'it was bitter to look at the white manse among the trees and know that I must never enter it' (LM, 5). Again there is a sense of voyeurism in the art of literary creation. Margaret, like a character in fiction, is unaware of the presence of the watcher.

At the climax of the improbable love story between Gavin and the gypsy girl, Babbie, Ogilvy begins to manipulate events. He tells Gavin the truth of the bigamous marriage and of the return of Margaret's husband, who had been presumed drowned. The story has its origins in a recurrent myth found in fishing communities, but Barrie inverts the pattern of Tennyson's *Enoch Arden*, and of Elizabeth Gaskell's *Sylvia's Lovers*. The husband, returning from the dead, does not sacrifice himself for the wife who has remarried. Having stayed away for his own pleasure, he delights in breaking up the new marriage. The description of Ogilvy and Margaret awaiting Adam Dishart's arrival has a powerful authenticity:

> After that we said very little. We sat at opposite sides of the fire, waiting for him, and you played on the floor. The harvesters trooped by, and there was a fiddle; and when it stopped, long stillness, and then a step. It was not Adam. You fell asleep, and we could hear nothing but the sea. There was a harvest moon.
>
> Once a dog ran past the door, and we both rose. Margaret pressed her hands on her breast. Sometimes she looked furtively at me, and I knew her thoughts. To me it was only misery that had come, but to her it was shame, so that when you woke and climbed into her lap she shivered at your touch. I could not look at her after that, for there was a horror of me growing in her face. (LM, 275)

Ogilvy's role as watcher, half in and half out of the story, accounts for some of the unease in Barrie's early fiction. It also alerts the reader to an important factor in his particular style and method. In *Sentimental Tommy*, Barrie dramatizes the artist's ability to adopt another person's role. Tommy ends by being unsure of his own identity. In *Margaret Ogilvy*, Barrie appears to enter into the consciousness of his subject, telling us 'that we were very like each other inside' (MO, 29): 'I see her frocks lengthening, though they were never very short, and the games given reluctantly up. The horror of my boyhood was that I knew a time would come when I also must give up the games, and how it was to be done I saw not' (MO, 28–9). This intense act of 'seeing' lends a tangible reality to the mother, envisaged at a moment of growth and change. It is followed by a startling parenthetic image in which the sleeping author watches himself as a boy: 'this agony still returns to me in dreams, when I catch myself playing marbles, and look on with cold displeasure' (MO, 29).

NOTES

1. *Letters of George Meredith*, ed. C. L. Cline (1970). II, 935.
2. G. Blake, *Barrie and the Kailyard School* (1951), pp. 72 and 66.
3. *Spectator*, 21 September 1889.
4. *Academy*, 26 May 1888.
5. Beinecke Library, Barrie Mss, A2/9.
6. Ditto, A2/10.
7. *Letters of Robert Louis Stevenson*, ed. S. Colvin (New York, 1889), II, 320–1.

CHAPTER IV

THE EARLY PLAYS

At the end of his life, Barrie more than once expressed a wistful regret that he had given up fiction for drama. He blamed Meredith and Henry Irving for persuading him to write plays, and Charles Frohman, the American impresario, for not letting him stop: 'I preferred writing books, and still think they were more my game, and remain uncertain that those good friends did not do me a great disservice' (GH, 267). That he initially found playwriting easy is confirmed by his friend and fellow-dramatist, Harley Granville Barker, in an article of 1910: 'It is interesting to note his [Barrie's] approach to play-writing. He seems to have taken to it quite casually, almost contemptuously, seeing at first neither difficulties to be overcome nor glory in overcoming them'.[1]

Such an attitude reflects current literary hierarchies. Prose was the dominant form of the mid-nineteenth century, and Barrie's own literary heroes were Carlyle and Scott, later succeeded by Meredith and Hardy. In the light of an aspiration to match the achievement of such writers, the drama seemed a lesser form of literature: 'In my first years... I never contemplated becoming a dramatist, and would have thought you harsh had you said it was the thing for me... The theatre and the oddities of its life drew me to them, but plays did not... the playwright was to me the one uninteresting figure of the whole clamjamfry' (GH, 267).

Barrie's interest in the 'oddities' of theatre life was

part of an intense preoccupation with ideas of illusion and with concepts of role playing. A perceptive critic, Allardyce Nicoll, compares him to Shakespeare in this respect, and asserts that Barrie's 'distinctive quality' lies in his 'acceptance of, and indeed emphasis upon, the fact that a play is no more than a figment'.[2] Barrie's notebooks are full of ideas for stories about the theatre, few of which he followed up. Around 1916 he wrote a horrifying short story, never published, about an actress whose stage self tries to take her over. Less alarming are the plays which explore the dual life-style of a popular performer. *Rosy Rapture, the Pride of the Beauty Chorus* (1915) and *The Truth about the Russian Dancers* (1920) were both written for women whom Barrie greatly admired, Gaby Deslys, the French music-hall artist, and the ballerina, Tamara Karsavina. In these plays he employs fantasy in order to express the inevitable conflicts when a woman of the theatre marries. A more successful treatment of the off-stage actress theme is the one-act play, *Rosalind* (1912), written within a realist mode. Here, a middle-aged idol takes a holiday from adulation by pretending to be her own mother. Only at the end of the play, when she is offered a new role, does she step out as a young woman once more. All three 'actress' plays represent different aspects of Barrie's life-long fascination with theatrical illusion.

Barrie's earliest contact with the drama came through the itinerant troupes who performed in Kirriemuir. Sam'l Mann's Tumbling Booth came twice a year, in summer for the Muckle Friday, and in winter for the 'storm stead', when the company were often trapped in town for weeks by the snow. Their performance is described in *Auld Licht Idylls*: 'the Fair Circassian, and the showman, who, besides playing "The Mountain Maid and the Shepherd's Bride," exhibited part of the tail of Balaam's ass, the helm of Noah's Ark, and the tartan plaid in which Flora

Macdonald wrapped Prince Charlie' (ALI, 14). 'The
Mountain Maid' was evidently a tableau with a
vestigial plot. Others were 'The Slave-Driver and his
Victims' and 'The Tragedy of Tiffano and the Haughty
Princess'. 'Tiffano loved the woodman's daughter, and
so he would not have the Haughty Princess, and so she
got a magician to turn him into a pumpkin, and then
she ate him' (ST, 201).

Kirriemuir 'herd-boys and others were sometimes
struck with the stage-fever' (ALI, 44) and ran off with
the players. In the manuscript version of *Sentimental
Tommy*, the hero's father is an actor who seduced Jean
Myles with his specious charms. She soon discovers that
life on the road is one of unrelenting drudgery. Barrie
was ambivalent about the romance of the stage. In a
deliberately deflationary passage in *Auld Licht Idylls*, the
narrator describes the citizens of Thrums 'plunging
through the snow or mud' at the 'heavy heels' of a
troupe who have come out into the streets to attract an
audience: 'It was Orpheus fallen from his high estate.
What a mockery the glare of the lamps and the capers
of the mountebanks were, and how satisfied were we to
enjoy it all without going inside' (ALI, 43).

As a Dumfries schoolboy, Barrie was an habitué of
the newly rebuilt Theatre Royal. A friend described
him as 'an inveterate "First Nighter" and "Pittite",
there can have been few (if any) of the plays that he
missed'.[3] In a short story of 1889, Barrie describes the
Dumfries theatre as 'like the town...small, and the
audiences are consequently not only well acquainted
with each other, but are as close together as though
they were in a drawing room'.[3] 'The Smallest Theatre',
an essay of the mid 1880s, gives a valuable glimpse of
the late nineteenth century provincial stage. In a
facetious vein, Barrie tells us that the set at Dumfries
began life as a cottage interior, but, as it wore out,
'obliged' for a number of plays, ranging from

Shakespearean tragedy to Dion Boucicault's *The Shaughraun*. The faces of the resident company became as familiar as the scenery, and, on one benefit night, the same actor started at seven with Hamlet, followed with Jacques and Macbeth, then played Romeo at half-past ten, and Handy Andy at eleven. As well as these truncated versions of the classics, the entertainment included songs and dances between the pieces, with Leah, the Jewish maiden, 'flung in as an extra' (GH, 58). Barrie's comment was tart: 'This kind of thing, I presume, is what is meant by the "all-round training" which actors got in the "palmy days" of provincial stock companies' (GH, 59).

On the theatre's inaugural night, 14 December 1876, Barrie saw J. H. Clyndes lead the resident company in three roles, Alfred Evelyn in Bulwer Lytton's *Money*, Dazzle in *London Assurance* by Boucicault, and finally Richard III. Each week brought a different group of plays, with occasional visiting companies providing further variety. The Gaiety Company from Glasgow performed *As You Like It*, the play which caught Barrie's imagination from the start and had a marked effect on his later work. The comic actor, John Lawrence Toole, played two of his great roles at the Theatre Royal, Paul Pry in John Poole's play of the same name, and Harry Coke in Clement Scott's *Off the Line*.

One night Barrie was allowed to sit behind the scenes, where the leading lady 'said to me in passing that her shoe, confound it, was loose as usual' (GH, 67). Fifty years later, he was still wondering: 'Is it possible that she meant I could tie those shoe-laces?' (GH, 67) Barrie and his friends became obsessed with the private life of the cast. They found out where the company stayed and what they paid for their lodgings. Their curiosity is echoed in *Sentimental Tommy*, where Corp Shiach ponders on the question whether or not the leading actress had a boiled egg for tea. The boys performed their own versions of *Paul Pry* and *Off the Line*, with Barrie taking a female role in the former. His first original play, *Bandalero the Bandit*, was a fifteen minute melodrama in six scenes in which the author played two pathetic but loyal characters, Smike from *Nicholas Nickleby* and Wamba from *Ivanhoe*.

When Barrie moved to Edinburgh in 1878, he was able to extend his theatrical range. Short of money, he was fortunate to find a congenial means of supplementing his income by writing reviews for the *Edinburgh Evening Courant*. Affecting a spurious maturity, he describes his first assignment, at the Blankton Theatre Royal, in a draft article written behind his notes on an Astronomy lecture, given on 4 January 1881:

> As my commonplace bk reminds me the piece on which I must make my maiden onslaught was one of those interminable comedies which may be, as their authors assert 'new & original' but which nevertheless bear to each other so striking a family resemblance. Justice but no favour was to be my motto — even this I find in black & white in my tell tale bk.[4]

Not all the plays were new. Barrie attended a performance of Dion Boucicault's Irish drama, *Arrah na Pogre or the Wicklow Wedding* dating from 1864, and saw two plays by Thomas William Robertson, *Ours* of 1866 and *School* of 1869. He thought *School*, which starred Robertson's widow, Cora Stuart: 'artificial tho' rather amusing...Most of the company wd need to go to school before they seek to act it'.[5] Boucicault and Robertson were leading dramatists of the mid-Victorian period. They eschewed the stock characters and situations of popular theatre for a more considered and realistic type of social drama. Robertson, a pivotal figure in the history of English drama, attempted to unify the tone of his plays, sometimes by centring them around a particular theme, epitomised in such titles as *School* or *Caste*. He also used carefully detailed domestic interiors. Robertson's work was taken up by Squire and Marie Bancroft at the Prince of Wales's Theatre in London, and they continued to woo a middle class audience with plays set in a recognisable social milieu.

Barrie's major plays fall within this tradition of 'society drama', although he can never be narrowly type-cast. His subject-matter is not readily confined within 'social' limits. The disappearance of *Mary Rose*, the enchanted wood of *Dear Brutus*, the islands of *The Admirable Crichton* and *Peter Pan*; all of these introduce a fantastic element after opening scenes in conventional domestic settings.

In his mature years, Barrie found success in drama rather than fiction largely because in writing for the theatre he could project himself into the separate roles of his characters without having to establish a realist context. His gift for dramatic dialogue took time to develop, and was never achieved without sustained concentration and constant revision. His five early plays, tossed off between 1891 and 1893, fail to create convincing characters or dialogue. They were trial pieces, exploring themes which were not repeated. Three of these first plays, *Richard Savage*, *Becky Sharp* and *Jane Annie*, were flops. Even so, Barrie gained experience through experiment in a buoyant market. At London's numerous theatres, relatively few plays had a long run of the kind considered commercially imperative today. Single matinée performances and double or treble bills of short pieces were a commonplace. The voracious demands of the late nineteenth century theatre provided an outlet for short and striking works not entirely dissimilar to that now provided by radio and television.

Barrie's first play, *Richard Savage*, was written in collaboration with Henry Marriott Watson. The subject was the eighteenth century poet of the title, and the result was a thoroughly inept four act drama, which only ran for one private performance in April 1891. As a costume drama, with abundant intrigue and a good deal of pseudo period dialogue, *Richard Savage* comes close to inadvertent farce. Numerous attempts to murder the gloomy and discontented hero are perpetrated by his mother's lover. Finally, after various escapes, Savage meets his end in touching circumstances. Barrie learnt the lesson and did not attempt historical drama again.

Collaboration can perhaps be blamed for the defects of *Richard Savage*, and for another of Barrie's early disasters, *Jane Annie or The Good Conduct Prize*, a piece of poor man's Gilbert and Sullivan, written with Arthur Conan Doyle, and first performed at the Savoy Theatre in May 1893. If *Richard Savage* fails through being over-solemn and turgid, *Jane Annie* is simply trivial, and met a deserved fate.

Barrie's third cul de sac was potentially more fruitful. This was *Becky Sharp*, an adaptation of the final chapters of *Vanity Fair*, set entirely in Becky's room at Pumpernickel. Barrie reduces Thackeray's narrative to a thin pastiche of the original. 'When a man dramatises his troubles begin' (L, 10) he later told his friend, Arthur Quiller Couch.

Becky Sharp was first performed as part of a triple bill accompanied by Thomas Hardy's adaptation of his own short-story, 'The Three Wayfarers', written at Barrie's suggestion. 'Plays and novels require quite different construction', he wrote, 'but the story-writer who is dramatic could become sufficiently theatrical by serving a short apprenticeship to the stage. There are such prizes to pluck for those who can stand on tiptoe'.[6] The message of the 'short apprenticeship' and of the 'prizes' was not lost on Barrie himself. Undeterred, he continued trying to find the right key to what he felt sure were immense possibilities.

Barrie wrote a number of magazine articles which probed the failings of the London theatre. In 'The Coming Dramatist', written for the *Scots Observer* in 1889, he criticized Henry Irving and others for relying too much on revivals of Shakespeare, and lamented the absence of good contemporary dramatists: 'By far the healthiest sign of the stage would be the appearance of new playwrights of distinction, and Mr. Irving seems to have given up looking for them'.[7]

When Barrie met Irving at the Garrick Club two years later and mentioned his own ambition to write for the stage, he was encouraged to submit a manuscript for consideration. A burlesque entitled *Ibsen's Ghost* soon followed.

Production of *A Doll's House* in 1889, followed by a spate of Ibsen productions in 1891, provoked a storm of indignation. Having seen Elizabeth Robins in *Hedda Gabler*, Barrie scribbled down his parody. Irving declined the play for the Lyceum, but persuaded J. L. Toole that it was worth putting on. After rushed rehearsals, it opened on 30 May 1891, as the second half of a double bill, with Irene Vanbrugh as Thea, and Toole as her grandfather.

The main target for Barrie's satire was *Hedda Gabler*. He continued the plot of Ibsen's play following Hedda's suicide. Tesman has married Thea Elvsted, who gradually assumes the character of her predecessor. Like many Ibsen characters, Thea has a guilty secret, in her case a propensity for kissing every man she meets. Her grandfather, like Mrs Alving in *Ghosts*, is driven to confess that the vice is inherited, and from himself. Ideas of female emancipation from *A Doll's House* are interwoven with motifs from *Ghosts* and *Hedda Gabler* to produce a burlesque version of an Ibsen plot. The climax comes in a passage of metamorphosis as Thea changes into Hedda's clothes and wig, while her grandfather appears as Ibsen.

In her analysis of *Ibsen's Ghost*, Penelope Griffin draws attention to Barrie's responsiveness to language. He echoes catch-phrases like Tesman's 'Just think of that now' to reveal Ibsen's dependence on significant repetition. Barrie's characters repeatedly exclaim 'Ghosts!', as a comic reminder of the Norwegian dramatist's gloomy preoccupation with the past. The play even refers to the conflict between Ibsen's early translators, William Archer and Edmund Gosse, imitating their often inelegant translations in such expressions as 'I know, I feel that as I have been in the past, so shall I be in the future'.[8]

Barrie rightly insisted that his parody could only work if played in a serious spirit. Absurdities must be played with a straight face.

> George: ... Tia, how many T's in 'tentative'.
> Tia (*indifferently*): Four
> George: And how many 'z's in 'influenza'?
> Tia: What does it matter, you take it all the same.
> George: Does 'civil' begin with 's'?
> Tia: Don't know, write polite.
> George: I will Hedda, I mean Tia, and is there a K in Christianity.
> Tia: There is nothing in Christianity.[9]

Ibsen's Ghost stays well within the bounds of good humour. Even so, as the years went by, Barrie felt some anxiety about it. In 1891, Ibsen's last plays were still unwritten. By 1928 Barrie would call him 'the mightiest craftsman that ever wrote for our kind friends in front' (CP, 491). Four years later, having just retrieved the manuscript of *Ibsen's Ghost* from the Lord Chamberlain's office, he speculated on how he 'could have made play, even for twenty minutes, with the dramatist I have always known to be the greatest of his age. Perhaps my soap-bubble was meant to fall upon his more weird idolators'.[10]

Following the success of *Ibsen's Ghost*, in October 1891, Toole bought the rights to Barrie's three act play, *Walker, London*, which opened at Toole's Theatre in February 1892. Four young people are spending the summer on a houseboat on the Thames, chaperoned by the mother and younger brother of one of the girls. The expectation that the two couples will marry is temporarily disturbed by the arrival of a barber, Jasper Phipps, who impersonates an African explorer. Phipps becomes involved with both girls, but nemesis, in the form of his fiancée, Sarah, is never far away, and the outcome is not in serious doubt. The plot, following a common comic pattern, derives in part from Barrie's novel, *When a Man's Single*. Here the elements are rearranged into a tighter form, revealing the very different way in which Barrie worked up material for the theatre on the one hand, and for his fiction on the other. Toole played the part for all it was worth, revelling in the scenes where Phipps struggles to maintain his disguise against ever mounting odds.

> Jasper:...Oh, I shot an elephant once! Oh yes, I did! I met the elephant in a forest, and I had an air gun with me, and I shot it. You can't shoot without a gun in Africa. You would have been surprised if you had seen the birds, the way they came down and pecked it. Hundreds of them!
> Bell: What kind of birds?
> Jasper: Oh, there were eagles and snipe — vultures, sparrows, canaries, turkeys and bull-rushes, the oof bird — they ate that elephant up and left nothing but the trunk.
> Bell: And what did you do with the trunk?
> Jasper: Oh, I had it packed up. No, no, I had the trunk made into a portmanteau. (CP, 23)

The elegant construction and lightness of touch of *Walker, London* contrasts with the laboured qualities of

Jane Annie and *Becky Sharp*. All were written at much the same time, but the far higher quality of the first probably reflects the time and trouble that Barrie took over it. Critics noted how quickly he was acquiring mastery in a new medium. 'When he was rehearsing Ibsen's Ghost, he had no idea what he wanted; dress and business he left alike despairingly to the company. But when he rehearsed Walker, London, he had precise views about every detail'.[11]

The play was an immediate success, Clement Scott in the *Daily Telegraph* hailed Barrie as the new Robertson, praising his craftmanship, his humour and his humanity. *Walker, London* ran for over a year, and represented Barrie's break-through in the theatre. So complete was his control of the structure that he was able to confine the whole play to one, highly original, set. Life on the houseboat is far from idyllic, and this neat and proficient play is punctuated by the sound of the slovenly cook smashing plates in the kitchen below. Recalling it eighteen years later, Granville Barker saw in it 'evidence enough of the extraordinary scenic inventiveness to be cultivated later'.[12]

Henry Irving had not forgotten Barrie, and he now commissioned him to write a play for the Lyceum. In August 1892, Barrie sent a three-act comedy, *The Professor's Love Story*, which Irving reserved for six months, and then declined on the grounds that it was too small for the Lyceum. He sold the rights to the actor, Edward Smith Willard, who opened *The Professor's Love Story* with considerable success in New York in December 1892.

The play is based upon the absurd premise that a distinguished scientist in his forties is so absent-minded that he fails to realize that he has fallen in love with his young secretary. Professor Goodwillie was first projected as 'Bookworm' in a notebook of 1890. In the play, Barrie combined 'Bookworm' with another old idea for a play, which he called 'The Self Made Woman'. She becomes the Professor's spinster sister, soured in her youth, when a letter of proposal failed to arrive from Australia. In the course of the play the misplaced letter is discovered. The lover is dead, but, as the notebook puts it, 'this softens her'.[13]

Like many of Barrie's later plays, the comedy revolves around the superior knowingness of the female. Well aware that the Professor loves her, the secretary, Lucy White, is a vulnerable figure in the hostile world of the Professor's family and friends. Among her opponents are the dowager Lady Gilding, pursuing the Professor for her own ends, and Lady Gilding's step-son, Sir George. A rich man, he decides to find out what the life of the poor is like by sending his family into the fields to work, wearing 'dresses such as those worn by the common things while harvesting' (CP, 85). The arrival of a 'gorgeous MALE SERVANT and PAGE BOY' with 'lunch-basket and champagne' (CP, 85), explodes the pretence. The useless and extravagant lives of the upper-classes are already becoming a butt for Barrie's trenchant satire, anticipating the sallies of *The Admirable Crichton*.

Written soon after Barrie's Thrums stories, the play makes use of Scottish characters and settings. In the sub-plot the maid, Effie, is courted by two young Scotsmen, Henders and Pete. Like T'nowhead's Bell, from *Auld Licht Idylls*, she intends to marry whichever suitor asks her first. The themes of love and courtship in high and low life are directly counterpointed in plot and sub-plot. The knowing but passive Effie is pursued by two men, while the ignorant Professor is the prey of two women.

The Professor's Love Story is the most Shakespearean of Barrie's comedies. Tullochmains is his forest of Arden, a place in which the strictures of city life can melt into pastoral idyll. From a position of superior knowledge the audience watches the network of deceptions and self-delusions unfold, and the dawning consciousness of the truth among the different characters. There is little psychological subtlety, but the stress on the passage of time, and the ideas of loss associated with Miss Goodwillie are new and more profound elements in his play-writing.

The critic William Archer, Ibsen's champion, thought the play trivial, but the craft appealed to the heart of a professional stage man, Henry Irving: 'You have a remarkable way of getting your characters off — always a difficulty with playwrights and players'.[14]

Between *The Professor's Love Story* and the end of the century, Barrie's only large venture in the theatre was the dramatization of his popular novel, *The Little Minister*, expanded from an outline made by his agent, Arthur Addison Bright. The play suffers from compression. The relationship between the narrator dominie and the minister's mother is suppressed. The heroine, Babbie, becomes Lord Rintoul's daughter, rather than his fiancée or ward. The effect of both changes is to remove all significant tension. A bright and cheerful drama emerges, lacking either mystery or originality. Performed at the Haymarket Theatre under Cyril Maude's directorship, with Maude's wife, Winifred Emery, as Babbie, *The Little Minister* was Barrie's first smash hit. From the London and American productions the author was estimated to have made eighty thousand pounds in ten years, a vast sum for the period.

Barrie's own opinion of *The Little Minister* was equivocal. He enjoyed the casting and the rehearsals, but, when he put together the Uniform Edition of his plays, he left it out. Another omission was his 'problem play', *The Wedding Guest*, which followed *The Little Minister*, opening at the Garrick Theatre in 1900. His choice of subject reflects a contemporary vogue for plays about women with a past. Oscar Wilde's *Lady Windermere's Fan* and Arthur Pinero's *The Second Mrs. Tanqueray* both date from 1892–93. The latter play moved Barrie deeply, and he would write later to the author, who became a good friend, 'the woman is a masterly study bound to hold her place in the annals of dramatic writing'.[15]

In its final version, as a four-act play, *The Wedding Guest* runs a predictable course of alarms and tensions. The drawing-room marriage of Paul Digby and his young wife, Margaret Fairbairn, is marred by the appearance of Paul's former mistress, Kate Ommaney, who has had a child by him. Barrie began his construction of the play with this scene clear in his mind: 'Scotch wedding — The other woman steals in while it is in progress'.[16] The second and third acts, which take place in Kate's humble lodgings, move towards Margaret's delayed discovery of the truth, and the play ends with Kate returning to her father, and Margaret sticking by her husband.

As ever, Barrie is most penetrating in his study of relations between the sexes, the weakness of men and the superior perception of women. Here is a memorable passage between Paul and Kate, their first dialogue after he learns of the existence of their child:

Paul: ...At least believe this, that had I understood I would not have let you go.

Mrs. Ommaney: I know, But oh, you were glad to be free! Can you deny it?

(Paul cannot answer)

Your heart leapt within you, did it not?

Paul: I was distraught with grief and shame.

Mrs Ommaney: But joy came in the morning!

Paul: You said you were going home — I thought of following you.

Mrs. Ommaney (bitingly): Did you go?

Paul: You asked me in the letter not to do so.
Mrs. Ommaney: How obedient a man can be
sometimes! (CP, 250)

Notebook entries on Grizel's despair for *Tommy and
Grizel* surround Barrie's original plans for the play, a
study in contrasts between the over-protected Margaret
and the heart-broken Kate. His feeling for the plight of
the unhappy woman owes much to his reading of three
admired novels, Fontane's *Effi Briest*, Meredith's *Rhoda
Fleming* and Hardy's *Tess of the D'Urbevilles*.

Although it ran for a hundred performances, *The
Wedding Guest* was never a popular play, and the
dramatist refused to sanction its revival. Its heavy and
humourless touch seems to have embarrassed him.
Some years later, in *Alice Sit-By-The-Fire*, he poked fun
at the intense 'triangular' plays of the Pinero school.
Two stage-struck young girls spend all their money on
tickets for the theatre:

> Ginevra. Amy, that heart-gripping scene when the
> love-maddened woman visited the *man* in his
> *chambers*.
> Amy: She wasn't absolutely love-maddened,
> Ginevra; she really loved her husband best all the
> time.
> Ginevra: Not till the last act, darling.
> Amy: Please don't say it, Ginevra. She was most
> foolish, especially in the crêpe de chine, but *we*
> know that she only went to the man's chambers to
> get back her letters. How I trembled for her then.
> Ginevra: I was strangely calm.
> Amy: Oh, Ginevra, I had such a presentiment that
> the huband would call at those chambers while she
> was there. And he did. Ginevra, you remember his
> knock upon the door. (CP, 601)

54 J. M. BARRIE

NOTES

1. H. Granville Barker, 'J. M. Barrie as a Dramatist', *The Bookman* XXXIX, No. 229 (Oct, 1910), 13.
2. A. Nicoll, *English Drama: 1900–1930* (Cambridge, 1973), p. 347.
3. Beinecke Library, Barrie Mss, A2/45.
4. National Library of Scotland, Ms, 6650.
5. Beinecke Library, Barrie Mss, A3.
6. J. M. Barrie, 'The Coming Dramatist', *A Tillyloss Scandal* (New York, 1893), p. 264.
7. Ditto, pp. 260–1.
8. J. M. Barrie, *Ibsen's Ghost*, ed. P. Griffin, (1975), p. 56.
9. Ditto, p. 19.
10. Ditto, p. 13.
11. J. A. Hammerton, *Barrie: The Story of a Genius* (1929), p. 172.
12. 'J. M. Barrie as a Dramatist', p. 13.
13. Beinecke Library, Barrie Mss, A2/13.
14. Laurence Irving, *Henry Irving* (1951), p. 565.
15. Letter of 12 Jan 1913, Beinecke Library, Barrie Mss, A3.
16. Ditto, A2/16.

CHAPTER V

SENTIMENTAL TOMMY

Of all Barrie's works, *Sentimental Tommy* is the most neglected. Barrie himself was well aware of its importance in his career. Responding to criticisms that he was writing too much and too fast, he made a conscious decision to take the time to write a mature and finished novel. He began work on 7 July 1893 and finished in late March or April of the following year. This was his first serious attempt to evoke the nature of boyhood in his writing, but it was a subject which had been long in his mind. In a draft article of 1884–5 he considered the attempts of other novelists, including Meredith, Margaret Oliphant and Thackeray, to create believable boy characters. Few matched up to his ideal, but he rated Traddles in Dickens' *David Copperfield* and Tom Tulliver in George Eliot's *The Mill on the Floss* as outstanding examples. If he judged other novelists by their skill in conveying the essence of a boy, Barrie himself is facing the ultimate test in *Sentimental Tommy*. The opening chapters are a tour-de-force. He achieves a truly remarkable presentation of that combination of heartlessness and vulnerability which he believed to lie at the heart of the child's consciousness.

In the first paragraph of the first draft, later deleted, Barrie demands that his reader should identify with his hero, and attempt a conscious analysis of self through the power of memory:

> Cast your mind back into its earliest years, and thro' them you will see flitting dimly the elusive

form of a child. He is yourself, as soon as you can
catch him. But move a step nearer, and he is not
there. Among the mists of infancy he plays hide
and seek with you, until one day he trips and falls
into the daylight. Now you seize him; and with
that touch you two are one. It is the birth of self-
consciousness.[1]

The novel opens with Tommy Sandys as a boy of
five, living in poverty with his mother in London. His
father is dead, and, during the course of Chapter 1, a
posthumous child, Elspeth, is born. His mother dies
when Tommy is eleven, leaving her children to be
brought up in Thrums by her former lover, Aaron
Latta. The novel ends with Tommy at the age of
fifteen, leaving Thrums to work as a herd-boy. By this
time, it is clear enough that Tommy is destined to be a
writer, which, as the narrator constantly reminds us, is
not a calling likely to bring him much happiness. Like
James Joyce in *Portrait of the Artist as a Young Man*, or
Thomas Mann in *Doctor Faustus*, Barrie explains the
artistic temperament through images of distancing and
coldness. The original manuscript of the first chapter
reads: '[Tommy] seems on the way to being an artist.
Alack!'[1]

Ideas for Tommy were in Barrie's mind at least as
early as the autumn of 1890, when he jotted down a
number of apparently isolated phrases in a notebook:
'Thrums in London', 'Magerful = masterful', 'The
Double Dykes'.[2] Then come longer passages about a
'Sentimentalist,' who seduces a young actress and treats
her like a slave. There is such a strong autobiographical
element in these notes that Barrie himself can hardly
have known whether they were really plans for a book,
or a commentary on his own predicament.

By the end of the notebook, plans for the
'Sentimentalist' novel are becoming confused with
another, and older, scheme, first taken up in 1888,

and described as 'The Illegitimate Child'. The illegitimate girl, although delightful, is cursed with hereditary sexual impulses, too strong to be denied. Barrie had not resolved the issue of whether the father or the lover should be the villain of the story, but he was convinced of the need for a tragic ending. The illegitimate child was eventually associated with another projected character, the alcoholic Painted Lady, who is sometimes the illegitimate girl herself, and sometimes her mother.

By 1892, the main outlines of the story had clarified themselves. The Sentimentalist had become Tommy, the illegitimate child, Grizel, and the Painted Lady, Grizel's mother. The tragedy was to lie in Tommy's relationship to Grizel, as much a realist as Tommy is a fantasist. Tommy was to be characterized by an inability to sustain any feeling for more than the briefest time. He is a sentimentalist because he can instinctively merge himself into the sensations of others, but never experience genuine emotion himself. Barrie implies that this is the sign of an artist. Throughout the novel, the commentating voice reminds us of Tommy's calling, and of the pain which that calling involves for any woman who has the misfortune to love him. Life is Tommy's raw material, and events and experiences are viewed from without, and transformed into art even as they are happening.

Sentimental Tommy carries on a continuous dialogue with itself, arguing out the case for its own validity as an imaginative creation. On one level, it has considerable power as a novel about childhood, and, specifically, about children who are subject to emotional and social deprivation. Underlying its apparent realism, however, is a discussion which considers how that realism is created, and what it means. In the course of the novel, much of Tommy's imaginative life takes place inside his own mind. Still a

c

boy at the close, his writing has been confined to letters and to school essays. Only in *Tommy and Grizel*, the sequel, will Tommy emerge as a published author. But what Barrie has to say about writing in *Sentimental Tommy* is, if anything, more telling than in the later novel, because here the act of writing is far more closely interwoven with the other themes of the book.

Long before Tommy himself can write letters, he encourages his mother to do so, and then watches her, fascinated by the physical actions which letter-writing involves. In *Sentimental Tommy* many letters are manipulative rather than informative. In hers Jean Myles is taking revenge on those who treated her cruelly. By presenting herself as wealthy and happy, the very opposite of the truth, she sets out to play a role, but without the subtlety her son will one day bring to the same art. Finally, the dying Jean is forced to write to a friend of Aaron Latta, telling him the truth, and asking him to rescue her children. This last letter, which ends the fantasy, is the means of moving the action of the novel from London to Thrums. Appropriately, Barrie also uses it as the means of introducing the second plot, that of the Painted Lady, who mistakes the letter for a message from the lover who has deserted her.

When Tommy himself becomes a letter-writer for the illiterate inhabitants of Thrums, he develops a gift for projecting himself into the feelings of those for whom he writes. It is on a par with his wearing another child's mourning clothes, so that he can experience bereavement. His cynical teacher, Cathro, comments: 'For though sometimes his emotion masters him completely, at other times he can step aside, as it were, and take an approving look at it. That is a characteristic of him, and not the least maddening one' (ST, 333).

Tommy not only lives through others, he can live

through literature. As his letter-writing can make him cry, so can he absorb himself into the world of Scott's *Waverley*, which he makes his friends and sister act out in their own recreations of the Jacobite rebellion. Grizel plays the part of Flora MacIvor, the highland heroine of *Waverley*. The account of the games in the Dell in Chapters 21 and 22 of *Sentimental Tommy* parallels the famous Chapter 22 of Scott's novel, where Flora plays and sings above a waterfall. Grizel's part is apt, since Flora loses Waverley in the end. Tommy too is appropriately cast as the fickle Young Pretender, attracted by women, but incapable of real love for them.

The gap between imagination and reality is exploited to great effect. Grizel, established as Flora MacIvor, has 'her face raised as if in wrapt communion with the heavens, and her feet tucked beneath her to avoid the mud' (ST, 256). She later breaks out of character to mend Tommy's clothes, while he is imagining himself 'rich apparel and ribbons rare' (ST, 259). Tommy's friend, Corp Shiach, a well-drawn contrast to the Cockney boy, Shovel, has to play multiple roles, even taking himself off for execution, a task which throws him into great confusion.

These passages are among the funniest in the novel, giving a true sense of the conviction with which children invent imaginary games, however absurd they may appear to outsiders. But in the end, the Jacobite episodes lead us round to the same question-mark as the other episodes of the novel. Here, in a work of literature, another work of literature is being acted out. What then is the status of literature, and of the imagination? While we laugh at the maid Gavinia's complete absorption in the first half of *Ivanhoe*, it still raises the question of escapism and retreat, particularly since we, like Gavinia and Tommy, are actually in the process of reading a novel.

There have been recurrent criticisms of the structure of *Sentimental Tommy*, which has been said to ramble, and to lack any overall unity. While this is not a tightly structured novel in the Jamesian manner, *Tommy* does have structural patterns and a far more organised shape than at first appears.

The novel is constructed as a series of significant episodes, each occupying several chapters, and revealing a further stage in the development of the hero's character. Between blocks, the story moves forward again, sometimes with considerable abruptness. In Chapter 19, for example, the narrator tells us that Tommy's best friend is Corp Shiach: 'It was fortunate', he goes on, 'that Elspeth liked Corp on the whole, for during the three years now to be rapidly passed over, Tommy took delight in his society, though he never treated him as an equal' (ST, 213). Barrie's method of construction is not dissimilar to that of D. H. Lawrence, of whose *Sons and Lovers* he was one of the earliest admirers. Nor does the parallel end with the use of striking episodes. In 1910, Lawrence compared his relationship with Jessie Chambers to that of Tommy and Grizel, and something of this found its way into his novel. Paul Morrell, like Tommy, is a talented boy in a limited working-class environment from which he has to escape.

Other novelists besides Barrie have successfully combined two separate themes in the same book, among them George Eliot in *Middlemarch* and Virginia Woolf in *Mrs. Dalloway*. Complementing the main theme of *Sentimental Tommy*, the nature of a young boy's imagination, is the sub-theme of the effect of a disjointed upbringing. Tommy Sandys, like Grizel, is a child of disgrace and misfortune. His mother, Jean Myles, had been betrothed to Aaron Latta, but threw him over when she became obsessed with Thomas Sandys, 'Magerful Tam'. Predictably, Sandys proved a bad husband. Barrie implies that Jean was a battered wife, and tells us that the infant Tommy expects any man he encounters to hit him. When her husband dies, Jean is left to bring up two children in dire poverty. The memory of these opening pages persists through both *Tommy* novels, however completely Tommy himself seems to have forgotten them. Barrie obliquely reveals the boy's desperate and continuous hunger, a hunger which his mother, deeply ashamed of their state, tells him to conceal:

> On his way up and down the stair he often paused to sniff, but he never asked for anything; his mother had warned him against it, and he carried out her injunction with almost unnecessary spirit, declining offers before they were made, as when passing a room, whence came the smell of fried fish, he might call in, 'I don't want none of your fish', or 'My mother says I don't not want the littlest bit', or wistfully, 'I ain't hungry', or more wistfully still, 'My mother says I ain't hungry.' (ST, 1)

Embarrassed by his 'sexless garments', Tommy only achieves masculinity when a pantomime principal boy gives him a cast-off costume, a further implication of uncertain sexuality. By contrast, the sex roles between the boy's parents, as seen through the eyes of his mother, present a copy-book differentiation:

> his masterful look fleid me, and yet it drew me against my will, and I was trembling wi' pride as well as fear when he made me queen...my will was no match for his, and the warst o't was I had a kind o' secret pleasure in being mastered. (ST, 107)

Tommy's memories of his father are less definite. He recalls the room where 'a man ate beef when a woman

and a boy ate bread' (ST, 21), and where the father's
'big soft chair' stood near to the fire:

> Of this man who was his father he could get no
> hold. He could feel his presence, but never see him.
> Yet he had a face. It sometimes pressed Tommy's
> face against it in order to hurt him, which it could
> do, being all short needles at the chin. (ST, 21)

For Tommy, the father remains 'the man who was
his father', or 'the man', and he is consistently unable
to envisage his face, or to give him a personality. He
has become an empty heap of clothes:

> What he did see was the man's clothes lying on the
> large chair just as he had placed them there when
> he undressed for the last time. The black coat and
> worsted waistcoat which he could take off together
> were on the seat, and the light trousers hung over
> the side, the legs on the hearthrug, with the red
> socks still sticking in them: a man without a body.
> (ST, 22)

Tommy is rarely able to re-assemble the patterns of his
early life with his parents. Significantly, his 'one vivid
recollection' (ST, 22) is of his mother's overwhelming
joy at the time of his father's death.

There is nothing conventional about Barrie's
treatment of the relationship between mother and child.
Within the barely furnished room, the two have a
world and a vocabulary of their own. Alone together
they use the Scots expressions which are part of the
mother's suppressed past. To Tommy, the Scots dialect
and intonation are part of a private language,
associated with the imaginative fantasy of his mother's
home-town. Barrie's remarkable ability to reproduce
speech allows him to move freely among a series of
effectively juxtaposed language patterns. Tommy who
speaks Scots with his mother, turns, like a bilingual

child, to an equally fluent Cockney, when he talks with his friend, Shovel. In this context, Tommy uses Scots dialect words as an aggressive weapon, where, later in the novel, he will find himself using Cockney terms for the same purpose in Thrums.

During the six years between Elspeth's birth and her own death, Jean Sandys struggles to hold down her job as a cleaner and dresser in a dancing-school. In the original manuscript the school is an ordinary one, and Barrie undoubtedly strengthened his work by the change. Through Tommy's uncomprehending eyes, the reader experiences the mixture of the common-place and the fantastic in the dancers' mysterious conversation. Once again, Barrie juxtaposes worlds and vocabularies, as Tommy listens to a language which has its own system of references, closed to those who have not the key.

Barrie deeply admired the work of George Meredith, and there are perhaps Meredithean echoes here, but, in the consistent use of a child's limited consciousness he comes much closer to Henry James, whose *What Maisie Knew* appeared a year later, in 1897.

Tommy's visit to the home of the lost child, Reddy, vividly conveys the deprived boy's responses to another way of life. Tommy, who has always lived in one room, cannot understand the purpose of rooms without beds: 'where on earth did they sleep?' The bookshelves make him look 'about him for the barrow' and the papers on the father's desk recall the quarters of butter which ought to be wrapped up in them. The father's dressing-gown is a 'brown blanket' to Tommy, and, fascinated by the desk, he fears that the man seated at it may end at the waist (ST, 29).

In the manuscript of *Sentimental Tommy*, Reddy is Grizel, and the over-dressed woman with her is the Painted Lady. When Elspeth and Tommy meet Grizel in Thrums, she shows them the penny with a hole which Tommy gave her in London. In the published version, Barrie cut out the real link between Grizel and Reddy, leaving only the imaginative one, that Tommy and Elspeth both suppose the two girls to be the same. One reviewer noted the apparently disconnected nature of the Reddy story, but Barrie must have decided that the coincidence was too improbable, or that Reddy must be a separate imaginative creation.

The climax of the first half of the novel comes when Tommy plans a special festivity for Hogmanay. Elspeth and he save up to buy three bridies (meat pies), an oatmeal cake and a hunk of kebbock (cheese), which have all come from Thrums. In Chapter 9, 'Auld Lang Syne', Barrie sets up a counterpoint between two levels of awareness; that of the children who expect their mother to enjoy this unexpected treat, and that of the exhausted and dying woman, for whom the well-remembered Hogmanay rituals, and the food which she is too ill to eat, represent an intensification of agonised regret.

For the reader, in possession of two viewpoints, the episode is tragi-comic, if irradiated with surprising warmth. After a rhetorical paragraph in which the narrator sets the word 'beautiful', used by Jean Myles' dying mother of her daughter, against the 'Gaunt slattern, fighting to bring up the phlegm' (ST, 96) which that daughter has become, he stands back from the scene, and affects to describe it dispassionately. The two groups fall apart, the mother to sit alone by the fire, and the children to play together. Even on this, almost their last evening together, mother and children do not communicate. The narrator briefly glosses their respective positions: 'she was as much engrossed in her own thoughts as they in theirs, but hers were sad and theirs were jocund — Hogmanay, like all festivals, being but a bank from which we can only draw what we put in' (ST, 102).

The early part of the novel is scattered with passages as good as this, several of them illustrating Tommy's increasing capacity for role-playing. The passage in London, where he pretends to be a reformed criminal in order to get a good meal, neatly balances the episode in Thrums when Tommy takes Corp's place, and describes how he feels during imaginary fits. Even at the most moving moments, as when his mother begs him not to become a masterful man like his father, Tommy is torn in two directions. He finds himself thinking: 'But I think I would fell like it' (ST, 119).

When their mother dies, Elspeth and Tommy are so excited that they are going to Thrums, the magic town of her reminiscences, that they fail to understand what is happening to them. Tommy agrees to keep his eyes shut at the funeral, so that he shall not see the town before Elspeth. He only looks up at the graveside: 'what he saw was his mother being shut up in a black hole and trying for ever and ever to get out' (ST, 135). Returning home, he discovers that Elspeth has been overcome by the same horrors:

> Tommy could never bear to see Elspeth crying, and he revealed his true self in his way of drying her tears.
> 'It will be so cold in that hole', she sobbed.
> 'No', he said, 'it's warm'.
> 'It will be dark'.
> 'No, it's clear'.
> 'She would like to get out'.
> 'No, she was terrible pleased to get in.'
> It was characteristic of him that he soon had Elspeth happy by arguments not one of which he believed himself; characteristic also that his own grief was soothed by the sound of them. (ST, 135-6)

Tommy and Elspeth's crushing disappointment with Thrums will have been foreseen by the reader. Tommy tries desperately to moderate Elspeth's discovery of the discrepancy between the Thrums of the imagination and the real town. Then, in a reversal of roles, Tommy finds himself reduced to frightening the Thrums boys with Cockney slang. Once away from it, the poor quarter of London begins to take the place of Thrums in his imaginative life.

Elspeth is the only person for whom Tommy consistently takes thought. At no point does Barrie suggest that Tommy is playing at loving Elspeth. This role is a real one, but its basis is his own security in her response. Her importance in the novel is not as a pious or unimaginative foil, but as a means of defining the nature of Tommy. When Tommy finally parts with Elspeth in *Tommy and Grizel*, his disintegration soon follows.

Grizel, the Painted Lady's child, presents us with a revealing parallel to Tommy. Both children have outcast mothers, living in isolation. Jean Sandys is a Scotswoman in London, the Painted Lady is an Englishwoman in Scotland. Both women have a different vocabulary from their neighbours. Jean Myles keeps her dialect words for her children, but the Painted Lady has no such control. Her use of words like 'sweet', 'pretty dears', 'lovely' is associated with her love of flowers, and with the 'aesthetic' arrangement of her house, all factors which set her apart from the rougher world in which she lives. They have left their mark on Grizel, whose speech is equally individual. 'Sweet', an overworked word in general, becomes a statement of identity on Grizel's lips.

Grizel's position is in many ways more disastrous than Tommy's. Like Dickens' illegitimate heroine, Esther Summerson in *Bleak House*, she has been forced into an unnatural maturity. The child takes over the role of parent, and is abused in return. The Painted Lady perceives Grizel as the primary cause of her unhappiness, and as a restraining force. Her mother's alcoholism exposes Grizel to a hostile world. When Tommy first meets her, she is trying to conceal a bottle under her clothes. Grizel's passion for domesticity expresses her need to create order. Unfashionable as her virtues are, she stands for human values in the novel.

In its published version, *Sentimental Tommy* is not always an easy novel for a reader to understand. In the opening pages this is because Barrie deliberately limits the viewpoint to Tommy's own, presenting an elliptical account of the world for which the adult reader must supply a context. If the manuscript of *Sentimental Tommy* is compared to the final text, it becomes clear that Barrie made more demands upon the reader's attention by deliberately omitting much explanatory material associated with the Painted Lady. Initially, he gave far more details of her father's discovery of her love affair, and of her Thrums lovers.

Some of the changes between manuscript and printed text reveal Barrie's growing determination to present Tommy as a specifically Scottish artist. In the original version, the children's games are inspired, not by *Waverley*, but by pirate stories. Even more striking are the changes in the account of the competition for the Blackadder essay prize. In the original, Tommy is trying to translate the Bible into Latin when he sticks on a passage from *The New Testament*: 'for in truth where the heart is, there alone shall the treasure be found'. While the other boys write, Tommy ponders the truth of the statement:

> 'Elspeth I aye kent that I could never do much at the learning, but I didna ken the reason. There it was, I couldna put my heart in't. Syne I saw in a klink that thae queer things I do was what my heart was in, and that instead o' stopping doing them I should go on at it till I find my treasure to

[sic]. The treasure you see means fame and sillar'.
'But did you find it?' inquired Elspeth eagerly.
'No I canna say I did, but find it I will, for I ken
now whaur ti look for't'.[3]

Barrie's alteration here draws together the Scots
themes, and associates the end of the novel with the
opening. In the revised passage, Tommy's imaginative
perception of Scots reveals him as a true artist. Having
begun his essay, Tommy stops because he cannot find
exactly the right word.

> He had wanted a Scotch word that would signify
> how many people were in church, and it was on
> the tip of his tongue but would come no farther.
> Puckle was nearly the word, but it did not mean
> so many people as he meant. The hour had gone
> by just like winking; he had forgotten all about
> time while searching his mind for the word. (ST,
> 437)

Tommy loses the bursary, but he reappears: 'tear-
stained but excited. "I ken the word now", he cried, "it
came to me a' at once; it is hantle!"' (ST, 440). If
Tommy has to go to a herding bothie, he has at least
avoided creative compromise.

Sentimental Tommy follows the pattern of a
bildungsroman, a form of a novel which, deriving
ultimately from Goethe, traces a young man's progress
towards maturity. Creatively, Tommy is now able to go
to full growth, but emotionally, the hero fails to
complete his progress, either in this novel, or in its
sequel, *Tommy and Grizel*.

The classic bildungsroman hero, from Goethe's
Wilhelm Meister onwards, is able in the end to select
the right marriage partner. Given another chance, the
hero can reach beyond his first, immature, decision. In
Tommy and Grizel, Tommy, not old enough to marry, is
torn between his sister and Grizel. Grizel, like a

bildungsroman heroine, is practical and realistic. Her qualities could provide the ideal complement to Tommy's capacity for imaginative abstraction. One crisis of decision comes after the Muckley Friday. With a packet of sweets in his pocket, and no money to buy another, Tommy knows that both Grizel and Elspeth are expecting to receive it. Tommy is rescued from the dilemma by the timely appearance of the Painted Lady, to whom he gravely presents the gift. Pleasing her daughter, he even manages to placate Elspeth by the splendour of the gesture. Later, when the Painted Lady is lying dead, Tommy's gesture is more instinctive.

> Her [Grizel's] eyes rested on him beseechingly, with a look he saw only once again in them until she was a woman; but his first thought was not for Grizel. Elspeth was clinging to him, terrified and sobbing, and he cried to her, 'Shut your een', and then led her tenderly away. He was always good to Elspeth. (ST, 353-4)

When Grizel runs away from Thrums, she asks Tommy to go with her. He prevaricates until the last minute, trying to achieve the impossible; to please Grizel by going with her, and Elspeth by staying behind. Tommy's gift for 'finding a way', is in essence a supreme gift for compromise. The dialect word 'swithering', perfectly conveys the hero's refusal to confront strong feeling. Having no emotional depth himself, he prefers manipulation and evasion when confronting it in others. The natural pull will always be towards his sister, whose admiration sustains the illusion of an unchanged world. When the reviewer for *Blackwood's* criticized Barrie for failing to direct his hero towards adulthood, he accurately identified the novelist's own intention:

> we hold it to be utterly immoral to treat of

boyhood as of a stage determinate and final,
irrespective of a future which shall not be a mere
sequence, but may be a vital regeneration,
absorbing the former qualities and enriching itself
while it changes them.[4]

Making frequent use of the word 'moral', the reviewer
goes on to attack Barrie for giving a false picture of the
artistic temperament, for implying that Tommy's
failings as a human being result from the nature of his
vocation.

The manuscript ending of *Sentimental Tommy* follows
Tommy from Thrums to Lookaboutyou Farm, and
describes his disgust at the loose talk and behaviour of
his fellow herdsmen. After three months, Tommy
collects Elspeth from Thrums and runs away with her
to London. The final sentence reiterates one of the
novel's most insistent themes: 'It should be remembered
that Tommy did this for Elspeth's sake'. The statement
is both true and false. Tommy believes that this is his
motive, but it is as much for himself as for Elspeth that
he runs away.

The revised ending, like Barrie's other changes to the
text, omits explanations. The novel ends with Tommy's
departure to become a herd-boy, and, when the story is
taken up again in *Tommy and Grizel*, he has arrived in
London. The reader is left to construct his own picture
of the effect of the bothie on the sensitive hero.

The final paragraphs, with their use of a winding
road to lead the hero out of the story, suggest the
influence of Thomas Hardy. Such effects are common
in Hardy's novels, where the characteristic use of a
path to take the reader into the landscape reflects the
influence of those Dutch painters in whom Hardy
delighted, Ruysdael and Hobbema. In Barrie's novel,
the road and the cart become the constituents of a
strong ending. Grizel does not take leave of Tommy

because of her jealousy of Elspeth. As the cart pulls away, Elspeth makes her way home, but Grizel climbs the hill to take a last look. Tommy, assuming that she is Elspeth, waves to her, and Grizel, knowing that Tommy will be 'unhappy if he thought Elspeth was too overcome with grief to wave to him' (ST, 452), stands in uncertainty:

> Then in a spirit of self-abnegation that surely raised her high among the daughters of men, though she was but a painted lady's child, she waved to him to save him pain, and he, still erect in the cart, waved back until nothing could be seen by either of them save wood and fields and a long, deserted road. (ST, 452)

NOTES

1. Beinecke Library, Barrie Mss, S45.
2. Ditto, A2/12
3. Beinecke Library, Barrie Mss, S45.
4. 'A New Boy in Fiction', *Blackwoods Magazine* CLX, No 974 (Dec 1896), 807.

CHAPTER VI

TOMMY AND GRIZEL

While Barrie was working on *Sentimental Tommy*, he realised that he could not complete the projected work in one volume. His solution was to write a second novel, *Tommy and Grizel*. Progress was very slow, and it was not until August 1899 that the book was ready. The two novels form a clear sequence, the first taking the hero from early childhood to the age of fifteen, the second from sixteen to his death in his twenties. There is less humour and exuberance in this second novel, and a narrowing of the range of subject-matter, as the plot revolves around the uneven and finally disastrous relationship between the now adult Tommy and Grizel.

The second novel, like the first, begins in London and then moves to Thrums. Tommy has taken Elspeth from Aaron Latta, as his father once took Jean Myles, and has returned to the scene of his parents' married life. He starts work as an amanuensis and ghost writer for a drunken hack, O. P. Pym. After six years, Tommy publishes a successful collection of idealised pieces, *Letters to a Young Man about to be Married*, known familiarly as *Sandys on Women*. Tommy has little experience of women, and interprets them according to his fantasies. As these correspond to their own dreams, the book pleases both parties. The irony is complicated by the narrator's generalisations about women, which only differ from Tommy's in their sparer language and greater pragmatism: 'The Elspeths of this world always have some man to devote himself to them; if the Tommies pass away the Davids spring up' (TG, 373), or, of Elspeth again: 'Like all true women, she always began in the middle' (TG, 29).

Tommy's personality provides continuity between the two novels, underlining the fact that the hero is incapable of real change. To the end, the narrator continues to remind us that Tommy is still a boy. For Grizel, however, the break between the two books is a period of growth. She has changed from an 'anxious girl' into a 'serene woman' (TG, 97). At the end of *Sentimental Tommy*, Grizel finds a home with Dr. McQueen as a housekeeper, assistant and adopted daughter. By the time of his death, a few years later, McQueen hopes that she has gained the necessary strength to suppress those passionate instincts which he associates with her fear of Tommy. McQueen anticipates her complete fulfilment as a mother, and asks his young assistant, David Gemmell, to protect Grizel by marrying her. Grizel, so like Dickens' Esther Summerson in so many ways, is being offered her Alan Woodcourt. But the circumstances are very different. It is implied that this would be a useful but loveless marriage. Grizel's warmth triumphs over prudence, but, like her mother, she is to find that yielding to love is self-destructive.

Barrie's original notes for Grizel's story lay stress on ideas of hereditary: 'a beautiful girl, but this curse of passion in her blood'.[1] Fortunately, the novelist resisted the temptation to make an overstrained connection between illegitimacy and sexual profligacy. He retained only the more general statements about Grizel's psychological inheritance from the Painted Lady: 'something in her blood that might waken and prevent her being a good woman' (TG, 43). On his return to Thrums, Tommy recognises the change in her, but also sees that her wistfulness has remained: 'Was it possible that the fear of him which the years had driven out of the girl still lived a ghost's life to haunt the woman?'

(TG, 97). This strain of imagery culminates in the narrator's unwilling admission that, after Grizel's nervous collapse, she seems to the Thrums community to be becoming more and more like her mother in appearance. McQueen's efforts to save her have been overthrown by Tommy's rejection of her love.

For much of the novel, the narrator carries on a dialogue with the reader, trying to balance the claims of the woman, Grizel, against those of the male, Tommy. In the end the narrator comes down on Grizel's side, while declaring considerable sympathy for the man who nearly destroys her. The repeated references to Tommy's immaturity and failure to grow up suggest that the hero is not responsible for his actions, or that his artistic temperament is to blame. The tone of these discussions, which often come in the opening paragraphs of the chapters, implies considerable intimacy, both with the characters and with the reader. Chapter 4, which introduces Grizel, begins:

> To expose Tommy for what he was, to appear to be scrupulously fair to him so that I might really damage him the more, that is what I set out to do in this book, and always when he seemed to be finding a way of getting round me (as I had a secret dread he might do) I was to remember Grizel and be obdurate. (TG, 41)

The final summing-up continues this air of open-ended discussion:

> But here, five and twenty years later, is the biography... You may wonder that I had the heart to write it. I do it, I have sometimes pretended to myself, that we may all laugh at the stripping of a rogue, but that was never my reason. Have I been too cunning, or have you seen through me all the time? Have you discovered that

I was really pitying the boy who was so fond of games that he could not with years become a man, telling nothing about him that was not true, but doing it with unnecessary scorn in the hope that I might goad you into crying, 'Come, come, you are too hard on him'. (TG, 428)

This is to treat characters as though they were real people, and to approach the subject-matter as though it were fluid, always capable of change or reassessment. The indefinite terms, suggesting the potential rather than the actual, are typical of *Tommy and Grizel* as a whole. 'Appear', 'might', 'set out to do', 'seemed', might do', 'was to' are all indications of a state of doubt and uncertainty.

As in *Sentimental Tommy*, the narrator underlines and reiterates Tommy's tendency to slip into an imaginary world. His fantasies, like Madame Bovary's, derive from romantic fiction, and, like hers, they threaten the less imaginative people by whom the dreamer is surrounded. Like the earlier novel, *Tommy and Grizel* contains an implicit commentary on the purposes and functions of fiction itself. Tommy himself has not the 'smallest instinct for story-writing' (TG, 25). *Sandys on Women* could have been called 'Bits cut out of a Story because they prevented its Marching' (TG, 27), says the narrator, and his *Unrequited Love* is a series of essays with no chapters, and no dialogue: 'yet a human heart was laid bare, and surely that was fiction in its highest form' (TG, 303).

Tommy's narrative gifts are given up to imagining romantic scenes for his own life and those of others. One of the clearest examples comes in Chapter 6, 'Ghosts that Haunt the Den'. Here, under the leadership of Tommy, Grizel, Elspeth and Corp attempt to relive one of the Jacobite Saturdays of their childhood. The use of indefinite and subjunctive expressions reflects the intangible nature of the past which the four are trying to recapture. The strong finite verbs which break into the uncertainty underline the inescapable truth that the past is beyond recall.

At the opening of the passage, even Grizel's pragmatism is lulled into hopeful and inconclusive statements about the nature of time:

> How often since the days of their childhood had Grizel wandered it alone, thinking of those dear times, making up her mind that if ever Tommy asked her to go into the den again with him she would not go, the place was so much sweeter to her than it could be to him. (TG, 71)

Time and the attempt to get outside it dominate the thoughts of the characters: 'Tommy would fain have had one of the Saturdays back' (TG, 71). Grizel asks Corp: 'But we can't turn back the clock, can we?' (TG, 72) As the scene gets underway, the uncertainty continues. In the face of the finite verb 'He took command', comes the sentence, 'He whispered, as if Black Cathro were still on the prowl for him' (TG, 72). Each of the party 'had to' do as Tommy said, until Grizel 'came to and saw with consternation that Tommy had been ordering her about' (TG, 72).

Grizel breaks the spell, her usual role in the novel. She is to 'break the spell' with dramatic force in Chapter 29, when she interrupts Tommy's seduction of Alice Pippinworth. Grizel, the ideal mother-figure, is also the hard voice of reason, the emanation of the anti-aesthetic ethos of Thrums. Rejoicing that she has broken the Jacobite spell, she still wonders 'was it with him that she was annoyed for ordering or with herself for obeying? And why should she not obey when it was all a jest? It was as if she still had some lingering fear of Tommy' (TG, 73).

The narrator, in directing our sympathy towards Grizel, is aware that he is not presenting a wholly attractive picture. Describing her reactions to Tommy's first book, the narrator says that Grizel looked 'as through a microscope for something wrong, hoping not to find it, but looking minutely... it was the writer of the book she was peering for' (TG, 74). She is irritated to discover that the subject is woman, and 'still more irritated on hearing that the work was rich in sublime thoughts. As a boy, he had maddened her most in his grandest moments. I can think of no other excuse for her' (TG, 74).

Another 'excuse' for Grizel can be found in the hostile views of Tommy expressed by the other male characters; Aaron Latta compares him to his father, and he is distrusted by Cathro, his old school-master, by the dead Dr. McQueen and by his brother-in-law, David Gemmell. Since Tommy prefers ingratiating himself with women, this dislike is predictable, but Grizel's doubts about him are based upon a mixture of instinct and common-sense. She wants to protect Tommy, it is the mother in her which reaches out to him, only to find that her own maternal instincts are dammed up in a sterile relationship. A deleted sentence may reveal Barrie's own judgement on his hero: 'What God will find hardest to forgive in him, I think, is that Grizel never had a child'.[2]

As in *Sentimental Tommy*, Barrie's use of language provides a key to the novel's meaning. The term 'magerful' or 'masterful' is associated with Tommy's father, and Aaron Latta turns naturally to the term when he tries to rationalise his dislike of Tommy himself: 'he had the same masterful way of scooping everything into his lap when he was a laddie' (TG, 58). Grizel's instinctive fear of Tommy's power over her parallels Jean Myles' reaction to 'Magerful Tam', but Tommy assures her that it is she, Grizel, who is masterful, and the novel provides some support for this startling suggestion. It is of Grizel, not Tommy, that the word is first used in the novel, when we hear that the old Doctor's patients complain about her 'masterfulness about fresh air and cold water' (TG, 46). A few pages later, when Elspeth speaks of something 'masterful' in Grizel's manner, Barrie substituted the word for 'cold and hard'[3] between manuscript and printed text. In the end, even Grizel begins to see herself in this way: 'She smiled when he [Tommy] told her to go on being masterful' (TG, 98). A careful reading of the novel suggests that Barrie intends us to see both characters as potentially dominant, and locked in a struggle for power. Like Meredith's sonnet sequence, *Modern Love*, *Tommy and Grizel* explores an unhappy relationship with considerable honesty. The episode in which Tommy, to prove a point, severely damages his own ankle, shows to what lengths the antagonists are prepared to go. Tommy longs for Grizel's admiration only because she is slow to give it to him. He fantasizes about her: 'looking longingly after him, just as the dog looks, and then not being really a cruel man, he would call over his shoulder, "Put on your hat, little woman; you can come"' (TG, 108).

The clash between Grizel and Tommy is, on one level, the archetypal one between creative man and domestic woman. A few years later, Bernard Shaw explored the same theme in *Man and Superman*. After the breaking of their unofficial engagement, Grizel believes that Tommy will be brought face to face with the real world. Instead, after his unsuccessful attempt to write political essays, he publishes his *Unrequited Love*, drawing on Grizel's unhappiness as his subject. Her letter to him aptly expresses her disgust:

> I think it is a horrid book. The more beautifully it is written the more horrid it seems. No one was ever loved more truly than you. You can know nothing about unrequited love. Then why do you pretend to know? I see why you always avoided

telling me anything about the book, even its title. It is because you knew what I should say. It is nothing but sentiment. You were on your wings all the time you were writing it. That is why you could treat me as you did. Even to the last moment you deceived me. I suppose you deceived yourself also. (TG, 304–5)

Grizel believes that, without the 'wings' and the fantasy, a real Tommy would emerge. The reader, however, is never clear about the nature of the 'real' Tommy. With no sense of a norm from which the fantasist Tommy is deviating, each of his roles is as valid for us as the others.

The narrator does at times attempt to give an objective picture of Tommy. In Chapter 1, adopting the literary convention that he is writing a biography, he pretends to take down O. P. Pym's reminiscences of the sixteen year old Tommy, with his rich voice, and noble forehead. The narrator then tells us that Tommy's voice was 'squeaky', and the noble forehead non-existent. 'No, all that Pym saw was a pasty-faced boy of sixteen years old, and of an appearance mysteriously plain' (TG, 4).

We are likely to trust the narrator more than Pym, but even he sometimes acknowledges failures of understanding. At the first moment of crisis in Tommy's engagement to Grizel, when Tommy begins to yearn for his freedom, the narrator comments that 'He knew what he was…as you and I shall never be able to know him, eavesdrop how we may' (TG, 194).

Tommy's gift for emotional transference lies at the heart of his success with London society women. Knowing what they are thinking, he tells them exactly what they want to hear: 'There was a sweet something between them which brought them together, and also kept them apart; it allowed them to go a certain length, while it was also a reason why they could never,

never exceed that distance; and this was an ideal state for Tommy, who could be most loyal and tender so long as it was understood that he meant nothing in particular' (TG, 33).

The novel is consistently critical of the speciousness of London and the south. Where the Thrums images are domestic or rural, those describing characters in London tend to be artificial. Tommy and Aaron Latta are compared to 'two mastiffs meeting in the street' (TG, 55); but 'a secret in Mrs. Jerry's breast was like her pug in her arms, always kicking to get free' (TG, 39). In the London chapters Barrie refers to the Souls, a group of high-society women who flourished at the turn of the century. Tommy's relations with women almost constitute a parody of their philosophy of loving friendship.

At an early point in the novel, Tommy finds himself making a proposal of marriage to a wealthy widow, Mrs. Jerry. His recurring nightmare is that he is coming out of church as a married man, but here he falls under the spell of his own performance. Tommy's inner thoughts, set in brackets, are juxtaposed to his spoken words. '("Take care, you idiot!"),' '("What am I doing!" he groaned)' and, finally '("I am lost!")' (TG, 36–7). He even envisages his sister, Elspeth, 'sickening and dying of the news' (TG, 38). Fortunately, Mrs. Jerry refuses him.

For all its apparent gaiety, the proposal passage contains the seeds of Tommy's downfall. The narrator tells us that 'the god of sentiment (who has a tail)' was 'perhaps, like cannibals with their prisoner ... fattening him for a future feast' (TG, 38). The imagery of rapacity continues, now transferred to Tommy himself. After going home: 'He was in splendid fettle for writing that evening. Wild animals sleep after gorging, but it sent this monster, refreshed, to his work' (TG, 39).

Barrie retrieves the term, 'monster' for Tommy later.

Chapter 24, which follows his failure to go through
with his marriage to Grizel, is headed 'The Monster',
and begins with an even more exaggerated picture of
Tommy's egoism:

> Tommy's new character was that of a monster. He
> always liked the big parts... 'There has been
> nothing like it', he assured Grizel, 'since Red
> Riding Hood and the wolf. Why can't I fling off
> my disguise and cry "The better to eat you with!"'
> (TG, 282–3)

As with *Sentimental Tommy*, the reader of *Tommy and
Grizel* is tempted by expectations of a comic ending. At
times, Barrie appears to be following a well-trodden
path, rescuing his hero from the shallow society of
London and taking him home to Thrums and the
woman who truly loves him. For a time, Tommy tries
to play the part: 'Assuredly he did love her in his own
way' (TG, 179); 'He soothed her, ah, surely as only a
lover could soothe' (TG, 181). 'He must have loved
her' (TG, 182); 'Oh, surely it was love at last. He
thanked God that he loved at last' (TG, 196). Each
apparent statement conceals a doubt, as Tommy's crisis
of identity overwhelms him: 'As he hesitated he became
another person; in a flood of feeling he had a fierce
desire to tell her the truth about himself. But he did not
know what it was' (TG, 178).

The comments of the narrator and the events of the
novel slowly make the reader aware that the happy
ending is not to be. Tommy can 'fall in love', but he
cannot 'love'. Even when the hero marries the heroine,
it is only in an attempt to assuage his guilt after she has
had a complete nervous collapse. All Tommy's efforts to
deny his true self eventually fail. Faced with a conflict
between his wife and his work, he gives way before the
stronger force.

Among the ideas for *Tommy and Grizel* in Barrie's

1892 notebook is a reference to the heroine's journey to Switzerland: 'Terrible night in rain spent by heroine at Lucerne (?) the day she goes to see hero there. It is chiefly terrible [because] she once so resourceful now could & can do nothing for herself'.[4] Grizel's precipitate journey to Davos, when she believes that Tommy is ill, is the climax of the novel. Her single-minded determination is juxtaposed to Tommy's philandering with Alice Pippinworth, as the reader recognises that the two are on a collision course.

Grizel's arrival coincides with the moment when both Tommy and Alice are on the verge of casting off their masks, one of the most overtly sexual passages which Barrie ever wrote. Again, the relationship between the sexes is conceived in terms of a shifting balance of power. 'He was a masterful man up to a certain point only' (TG, 353), the narrator reminds us. Alice is the stronger, but, as the scene proceeds, sexuality begins to stir in her. Barrie's imagery combines ideas of animal strength and of performance. 'He was astride two horses, and both were at the gallop' (TG, 353). Tommy's rich platitudes suddenly take off into a 'frenzy of passion . . . he meant every word of it' (TG, 354).

Like the love duet in Wagner's *Tristan and Isolde*, the passage ends in frustration. The lovers become aware of another person in the room, Tommy strikes a match, and the light reveals the sleeping Grizel. She disappears, and, for sixty hours while he searches for her, Tommy abstains from sentiment, only to slip back into it when explaining to fellow-tourists that he has been shocked by a (wholly fictitious) death notice in the newspaper: 'It was the nobler Tommy, sternly facing facts, who by and by stepped into the train' (TG, 362), but throughout the whole journey to Thrums his mind is filled with fantasy pictures.

After Tommy's marriage to Grizel, and her recovery, Tommy is lured back to Alice Pippinworth. Barrie's source for this whole episode is *Hedda Gabler*, the play which he had once parodied in *Ibsen's Ghost*. Tommy's role is that of Eilert Lövborg in the original play. A brilliant, but weak man, Lövborg loses the manuscript of his new book. It falls into the hands of the destructive Hedda, who burns it. Lövborg, searching frantically for the manuscript, is shot accidentally. The parallels with *Tommy and Grizel* are very striking. Tommy is drawn to Alice, not because he loves her, but because he believes that she has his missing manuscript. Alice, realising that he cares more for the book than for herself, destroys it. Tommy, unable to resist her taunts, is accidentally hanged as he climbs a fence towards her.

Ibsen's manipulation of the themes of creativity in *Hedda Gabler* is amongst his finest and most controlled dramatic achievements. Barrie's borrowing results in a more confused picture, but one which draws upon the same associations between the child and the work of art. The marriage of Tommy and Grizel is unconsummated. Grizel believes that a child should not be born to parents when only one loves the other, and there is an implicit suggestion that Tommy's vocation as an artist inhibits his potential as a father, another prominent theme in Ibsen's later plays.

Tommy's grotesque death drew upon a real event in Kirriemuir legend. Barrie writes about it in *Auld Licht Idylls*, and then, in a notebook entry of 1890, relates it to his Sentimentalist hero: 'Death might come to man as like hawker hanged by his pack when the lad weary of his iniquity (or he might live on)'.[5] There is touch of the gothic in the manner of Tommy's end. When he delivers a panegyric to the memory of Dr. McQueen, a man whom he never liked, the grateful Grizel gives him the Doctor's overcoat. As Tommy climbs the fence, in pursuit of the mocking Alice, he slips. Protecting Grizel to the last, the dead man gains a posthumous victory as

the collar of his coat catches on a spike and chokes
Tommy to death.

NOTES

1. Beinecke Library, Barrie Mss, A2/12
2. A. Birkin, *J. M. Barrie and the Lost Boys* (1979), p. 40.
3. Beinecke Library, Barrie Mss, T65.
4. Ditto A2/14.
5. Ditto A2/12.

CHAPTER VII

BARRIE AND THE THEATRE: 1902–1917

The Wedding Guest marks the end of Barrie's apprenticeship in the theatre. 1902, the year of *Quality Street* and *The Admirable Crichton*, witnesses his advent as a mature dramatist. Fiction had been temporarily shelved in the interests of his new-found career. In 1905, Barrie told Quiller-Couch: 'I see plainly that one can't write plays and books alternately, or anything of that kind. One's ideas all get into the way of seeking for the one outlet, and so at present they form with me into acts. I never find myself wondering, should this be a story or a play. If it makes for the one, it couldn't to me make for the other' (L, 18).

'What lured me on', Barrie commented in 1930, 'was that the writing was in dialogue, which fascinated me from the moment I fell into it and found that I could swim' (GH, 267). A slightly different emphasis emerges in the opening stage direction written in 1919 for the Uniform Edition af *Alice Sit-By-The-Fire*. Telling us that Amy Grey keeps a diary, Barrie continues:

> so we could peep over her shoulder, while the reader peeps over ours. Then why don't we do it? Is it because this would be a form of eavesdropping, and that we cannot be sure our hands are clean enough to turn the pages of a young girl's thoughts? It cannot be that, because the novelists do it. It is because in a play we must tell little that is not revealed by the spoken words; you must ferret out all you want to know from them,

although of course now and then we may whisper
a conjecture in brackets. (CP, 597)

When Barrie began to 'swim', he found that
dramatic dialogue enforces economy, and obviates the
need for direct comment on the part of the narrator.
After completing *Tommy and Grizel*, he felt that prose
offered too many opportunities for the expression of an
increasingly dark view of life. Experience must be
controlled by humour: 'I fancy I try to create an
artificial world to myself because the one I really
inhabit, and the only one I could do any good in,
becomes too sombre. How doggedly my pen searches
for gaiety. My last chuckle will be got from watching it'
(L, 21).

Barrie's contribution to British drama did not include
much formal experiment, nor was he particularly
interested in developments in contemporary theatre. In
his full-length plays the relationship of the acts to each
other is as well-defined as that of the beginning of the
play to the end. He even contrives to stay within an
act-structure in *Peter Pan*, where his subject-matter
might have suggested the creation of a new mode.
According to Harley Granville Barker, Barrie scarcely
recognised the restriction which the contemporary
theatre represented: 'he went on as he had begun, his
fancies wedded — and at times incongruously — to a
realism of method'.[1] Barker characterises Barrie's more
experimental works as 'masques', referring specifically
to *Peter Pan* and *A Kiss for Cinderella*. The term could
also be applied to a wide range of Barrie's ephemera,
where, released from the straightjacket of the well-made
play, he frequently employs such devices as ballet and
mime.

For Barrie himself, these experiments were nostalgic
rather than progressive. *Pantaloon*, subtitled *A Plea for
an Ancient Family*, of 1905, is a conscious revival of the
Victorian Harlequinade, far removed from its origins in

the Italian improvised drama, the Commedia del Arte. Barrie was fascinated by the figure of Harlequin, and devised a mime, *The Origin of Harlequin*, first for an actors' benefit performance, and then as part of his musical, *Rosy Rapture*, of 1915. These later experiments, like *The Truth About the Russian Dancers*, of 1920, must reflect the ballet mania which followed the arrival of Diaghilev in London in 1910, but they also confirm Barrie's interest in working with dance and music as well as with stage dialogue.

In the Preface to *Pantaloon*, Barrie compares the popular and modern theatre. Pantaloon 'would have scorned to speak words written for him by any whippersnapper; what he said and did before the footlights were the result of mature conviction and represented his philosophy of life' (CP, 581). *Punch: a Toy Tragedy*, of 1905, burlesques Bernard Shaw's *Man and Superman* by comparing the theatre of ideas to another popular survival of the Commedia, the Punch and Judy show. Barrie's Punch is ousted by The New Man, dressed like Granville Barker in his role as Jack Tanner.

Barrie's own philosophy as a playwright retains some vestiges of the Commedia tradition. An inveterate attender of rehearsals, he was always prepared to listen to the actors, and, if appropriate, to change his mind. A Barrie play was a collaboration between cast, director and playwright: never finally completed, the texts were always open to revision.

After 1910, Barrie ceased to be a regular theatre-goer:

> My not going often to the theatre is not because I don't like it, but because the things I like best about it can be seen without actually going in. I like to gaze at the actors, not when dressed for their parts, but as they emerge by the stage-door. I have never got past the satisfaction of this and it is heightened when the play is my own. (S, 55)

Barrie once confessed that a text-book on playwriting seemed to him 'so learned, and the author knew so much, and the subject when studied grew so difficult that I hurriedly abandoned my inquiry' (GH, 268). He believed that the writing of plays was intensely personal, and he played down the significance of technique, rather as a photographer might disparage the importance of his equipment. For this reason, he was inclined to dismiss the last two acts of *What Every Woman Knows* as insufficiently inspired: 'The first act I always thought really good and the second also as a whole (with the English ladies to spoil it a bit). The rest is rather of the theatre somehow, ingenious enough but not dug out of myself. It isn't really the sort of man I am' (L, 21).

In the initial stages of planning a major play, Barrie would usually spend months, even years, in revising the text, refining and condensing it. His aim, he said 'was simply to make everything clear to myself in the hope that this would clear a way for the spectator' (GH, 268). Different plays presented particular difficulties, but they were usually concentrated at the end of the play. The final act of *The Admirable Crichton* was altered several times, that for *Peter Pan* did not take its eventual form until the 1920s. Changes made to the end of *Mary Rose* completely altered its effect. Of one projected play, never written, Barrie remarked that the first and second acts would be easy enough, but that he couldn't see his way into a third. *Shall We Join the Ladies?*, of which only one act was ever completed, is the tantalizing product of a similar dilemma. Perhaps for this reason, Barrie began writing *Dear Brutus* and *The Admirable Crichton* with the third act.

Planning a play in 1906, Barrie decided to set the scene and establish the background in the first act. The second would take place some years later, and would introduce a radical change in circumstance — in this case the death of the protagonist. In the problematic third act, it was to be discovered that he was still alive, with resulting complications.

A glance at Barrie's full-length plays will show how general this pattern was, with the 'change in circumstances' often provided by the passage of time. In *Quality Street* the gap between the first and second act is ten years, in *What Every Woman Knows*, *Little Mary* and *Mary Rose* five or six. If it narrows to two months in *The Admirable Crichton*, the change from Mayfair to a desert island is radical enough. The play is directly analogous to *Peter Pan*, which moves from Bloomsbury to the Never Land in a single night. *Dear Brutus* accomplished the 'change' by taking the characters into a magic wood, another world where they can enjoy a 'second chance'.

While Chekhov introduces new characters at the opening of the play, and then takes his disturbing outsiders away at the end, Barrie's characters more often than not make the journey back to the starting point. At the opening of *Quality Street*, Phoebe Throssel is waiting for a proposal from Valentine Brown. At the end, having turned herself into the imaginary Miss Livvy and back again, she actually receives a proposal. The return is not always so straightforward or so happy; it can imply exclusion. Crichton's talents are once more damned up by society, Dearth in *Dear Brutus* loses his 'might-have-been' daughter in the wood.

Those plays which are most optimistic in outlook suggest that some characters will grow through experience. Valentine Brown comes to recognise a love for which his younger self was not prepared. John Shand, in *What Every Woman Knows*, learns that he has been dependent upon his wife's talents, and he begins to laugh. Against this must be set Barrie's strongly held belief that people do not change. Of those who go into Lob's Wood, few will be altered by the experience. The

D

return of Mary Rose confuses and upsets her family. The aristocrats in *Crichton* simply resume their earlier roles, indolent, pampered and useless.

THE ADMIRABLE CRICHTON

Barrie's two plays of 1902, *Quality Street* and *The Admirable Crichton*, are an oddly assorted pair. *Crichton* is full of ideas and brilliantly sharp dialogue, where *Quality Street* is a pleasant diversion on a simple theme. Barrie had already drawn upon the two genteel sisters who kept a school in Kirriemuir for *Sentimental Tommy*, and now he incorporated them into a play, set in the Napoleonic period, about a woman who dresses as her younger self, and wins back her lover.

The two plays do, however, share a theme, that of role and reality. Crichton is the 'best man among us' (CP,418), but, while he is a butler, no-one will notice it. When Phoebe Throssel dresses as a girl ten years younger than herself, she is casting off the role of a middle aged spinster which society has thrust upon her. Her 'Miss Livvy' side is still in existence, but is buried under an exterior which looks 'not ten years older but twenty, and not an easy twenty' (CP, 290).

Ellaline Terriss, the original Phoebe Throssel, describes the care lavished on the set of *Quality Street*. The designer, Edwin Lutyens, and Barrie worked on it together, both greatly concerned with historical accuracy: 'even down to such small items as the velvet glove which hung next the fireplace for the handling of the Georgian tongs'.[2]

Barrie made similar demands about the accuracy of the set for *Crichton*, and here the problems proved to be more serious. The structure of the four-act play reflects its subject. Lord Loam's elegant house in Mayfair is the scene of the first and last acts, while the second and third take place on the desert island where Crichton proves to be the natural leader. Irene Vanbrugh, the first Lady Mary, describes the 'mechanical difficulties' which these changes of scene involved. 'In one scene there was the clearing of a patch on a desert island. The lighting of a log fire, a pot to be brought to the boil at a given moment, all needed very careful timing. The properties were extremely original and had to be made with the greatest care in every detail to give the true impression of hand-made efforts'.[3]

The problems of staging finally resulted in a strike of the theatre staff, which put the first night in jeopardy. In the event, the master craftsmen from other London theatres rallied round the producer, Dion Boucicault, and the play got off to a triumphant start. These conflicts in the wings, as was noted at the time, provided an ironic twist to the play itself, which could be seen as a plea for better understanding between classes.

In the first act, Lord Loam's household presents us with a class-dominated hierarchy, the peer and his three daughters at the top and the 'odds and ends', the stable-boy, the page and the kitchen wench, at the bottom. On intermediate levels come the upper servants: the butler, Bill Crichton, and the three ladies' maids, of whom even Lord Loam is nervous.

Once a month, Lord Loam, a mildly radical peer, presents an ineffectual challenge to the system by treating his servants as 'equals'. The result is a stilted and uneasy tea-party, smacking of condescension. Barrie's notebook shows that he had in mind the behaviour of Rosalind, the radical Countess of Carlisle. The embarrassment produced by the encounter results in a scene of high comedy. Crichton is among the strongest opponents of the tea-party scheme, but he is prevented from complaining by his respect for his employer. When Lady Mary asks him:

Lady Mary: I wonder — I really do — how you can remain with us.

> Crichton: I should have felt compelled to give notice, my lady, if the master had not had a seat in the Upper House. I cling to that. (CP, 354)

Crichton, an undeviating conservative, does not believe in half-measures. It is 'natural' to him that one should lead and others obey. The second and third acts prove the soundness of his judgement. On the island, Lord Loam, his daughters, and his nephew, the Hon. Ernest Woolley, happily take up subsidiary roles. They have little or no inherent quality, and in England they depend upon social rigidities for their position. When different virtues are needed, the practical Crichton becomes 'the Guv', and Eliza or Tweeny, who is the best cook, becomes an attractive proposition. Crichton organises the installation of electric light, dams up the river, and begins to comport himself like any other nouveau riche entrepreneur.

When Lady Brocklehurst cross-examines Crichton about social distinctions on the island, he is able to give an entirely honest answer, because, in a certain sense, nothing had changed:

> Lady Brocklehurst (sharply): Well, were you all equal on the island?
> Crichton: No, my lady. I think I may say there was as little equality there as elsewhere. (CP, 416)

The Admirable Crichton provokes a number of questions. How serious is Barrie's criticism of the class system, or of the aristocratic way of life? Like all the best comedies, it lifts up a disturbing mirror to human nature. When the audience is laughing most loudly, Barrie is often (like Oscar Wilde) telling it the truth about itself. On the island, Ernest, the reformed man about town, proposes to Tweeny, the one-time maid. His reply to her refusal is a wicked description of marriage:

Ernest (putting his case cleverly): Twice a week I should be away altogether — at the dam. On the other days you would never see me from breakfast time to supper. (*With the self abnegation of the true lover.*) If you like I'll even go fishing on Sundays. (CP, 389)

Some of Barrie's wittiest barbs are aimed at leisured indolence. Lady Mary is 'exhausted' by trying on engagement rings. She and her sisters cannot dress without help, and the idea of sharing a lady's maid fills them with horror. Granville Barker probably got it right when he described *Crichton* as a story 'eminently to have been written by a Scotsman living in luxurious snobbish England'.[4]

One of the startling revelations of the third act is the entry of the three girls. Dressed in male costume, and fresh from fishing or hunting, they are healthily free of the constricting pressures of society life. Lady Mary (now Polly) appears as a 'splendid boy, clad in skins...she carries bow and arrows and a blow-pipe, and over her shoulder is a fat buck, which she drops with a cry of triumph. Forgetting to enter demurely, she leaps through the window' (CP, 390).

At first glance, this is the heroine as Diana, the huntress, but Shakespeare's Rosalind provides an even closer parallel. In moving from the corrupt world of the court into the Forest of Arden, Rosalind changes into man's clothes. In a romantic comedy, changes of role are a means by which love can flourish. At the end of *As You Like It*, the good characters return to the court, cleansed of the usurpers. In *The Admirable Crichton*, the comedy is muted by disillusion. Crichton himself is the usurper of Lord Loam's role, and, in the final act, when clothes, names, and styles are changed once more, this change is accomplished in the service of sterile convention.

Even at this late stage, Lady Mary feels drawn towards the natural world: 'despite her garments it is a manly entrance...Lady Mary thoughtlessly sits like a boy...she seeks to draw his attention by whistling' (CP, 407). Lady Mary is to marry the brainless peer to whom she was originally engaged. His matching 'misalliance' with her former maid, Miss Fisher, is to be overlooked as 'natural' in a man, where her relationship with Crichton, if known, would be a social disaster. Marriage to Lord Brocklehurst will apparently be a sexual disaster, and productions usually suggest that Crichton is Lady Mary's natural mate.

It is by no means certain that this is precisely what Barrie meant. At the height of their relationship on the island, Crichton recites to Mary four lines from W. E. Henley's poem, 'To W. A.'. They are not lines which imply any possibility of an equal relationship:

> Or ever the knightly years were gone,
> With the old world to the grave,
> I was a *king* in Babylon,
> And you were a Christian slave. (CP, 398)

Barrie had apparently never read or seen Strindberg's *Miss Julie*, where the valet, Jean, seduces his employer's daughter, reversing the social balance between them by asserting his sexual domination. In contrast to Strindberg's play, Barrie's 'fantasy', while raising the issue of the lady and the servant, steers clear of any further discussion of 'shocking' issues. But, in avoiding the presentation of passion, the dramatist leaves the audience uneasy. Three days before the first production, Dion Boucicault expressed his concern about the scene where Lady Mary waits upon her lord and master, Crichton. In Irene Vanbrugh's eyes, Barrie 'made him treat Lady Mary as he might have treated a pretty waitress. The play had become so big and was so full of humanity that this treatment seemed to strike a wrong note'.[5] Barrie, always sensitive to the wishes of director and cast, went away and re-wrote the scene overnight. He came back with what we have today, and what seemed to Irene Vanbrugh 'a scene full of fancy, poetry and true romance'.[5]

The change may have falsified Barrie's intention by making Crichton too sympathetic. It certainly helps to confuse the audience's reactions to the final act. If we were sure that Crichton is Lady Mary's one true love, the end of the play could seem tragic, but Barrie does not allow the audience such certainty. Lady Mary is exceptional among Barrie's heroines in not proving herself of superior insight and perception. The much revised final exchange is deliberately equivocal:

> Lady Mary: To wish you every dear happiness.
> Crichton (an enigma to the last): The same to you, my lady.
> Lady Mary: Do you despise me, Crichton? (The man who could never tell a lie makes no answer.) I am ashamed of myself, but I am the sort of woman on whom shame sits lightly. (He does not condradict her.) You are the best man among us.
> Crichton: On an island, my lady, perhaps; but in England, no.
> Lady Mary (not inexcusably): Then there is something wrong with England.
> Crichton: My lady, not even from you can I listen to a word against England.
> Lady Mary: Tell me one thing: you have not lost your courage?
> Crichton: No, my lady.
> (She goes. He turns out the lights.) (CP, 418–9)

The development of Ernest Woolley is a shallower version of that of Lady Mary. As a young man about town, he affects witty epithets, which suggest that both his Christian name and surname were chosen with care.

On his return from the island, Ernest writes a dishonest account of the adventure, attributing Crichton's achievements to himself, and relegating the butler to a footnote. On the island, between these two low points, Woolley changes considerably. He becomes strong and athletic, and epithets are abandoned for a hard-working life. As in the case of the other upper-class characters, we may doubt whether his return home is to his advantage.

The disappearance of the servants' hall may have reduced the play's sharpness as a comedy of manners, but it has clarified the underlying questions about inequality of opportunity. The audience are easily convinced that Crichton is the 'best' man, because the opposition is so mediocre. Only the cricketing parson, Treherne, with his kindness and genuine modesty, restores some of the moral balance to the upper-class, for Crichton is notably without either virtue.

The butler is an ambiguous hero. By the third act, his genius for man-management has led him to separate himself from his companions and to demand a return to traditional patterns. He eats alone, and Treherne uneasily notices Crichton's love for sets of plates and hairbrushes, made from local materials. An undeveloped strand of Act Three suggests an even more sinister aspect of Crichton's role. He begins to wear a regal robe and to affect magnificence, revealing a private preoccupation with becoming a king. His nobility in signalling to the rescuing ship might well be played as *folie de grandeur*.

Here lies the crux of the play's ambiguity. For all its clarity of presentation, *The Admirable Crichton* does not provide the audience with a conclusive argument. The play remains provocatively open, and the dramatist's repeated changes to his text reflect an inherent uncertainty in his own response to the sexual and social issues with which his comedy is concerned. A notebook entry shows that this open-endedness was deliberate:

> Butler a rather tragic figure — cd. be pathetic but perhaps best end comedy — He is rubbing his hands together as curtain falls. No other indication as to how play is to end. Polly has said wd stick to him whatever happened. He But wd I stick to you.[6]

In the version presented at the earliest performances, the butler plans to leave service and to take over a pub in the Harrow Road. This detail was removed for the 1920 revival, when Barrie wrote a new fourth act where Crichton 'was made to express a deal of dissatisfaction with the inequalities and absurdities of English life. Further, he was made not only to foresee the great war, but to prophesy that when it came all the Bill Crichtons would get their chance'.[7] The change was not generally seen as an improvement, and this passage too was subsequently removed.

As a servant too talented for his post, Crichton has been compared to Henry Straker, the chaffeur and inverted snob is Shaw's *Man and Superman*, published in the following year. Straker, however, remains aggressively cockney, where Crichton's speech is restrained and formal. Only Tweeny with her 'its me what alters' and 'I does them up when they goes to parties' (CP, 361), speaks anything other than the King's English. Straker's association with the motor car suggests, like Crichton's development of electric light, an ability to adapt to a more technical future. Crichton's badge of office, however, is an obsequious wringing of the hands, a symbol of servility in the play. As Crichton stops doing it, Lady Mary begins, and then, at the moment of rescue, Crichton reverts: 'By an effort of will he ceases to be an erect figure; he has the humble bearing of a servant. His hands come together as if he were washing them' (CP, 403).

Barrie called Crichton a 'fantasy', and like many
fantasies or Utopias, it is as much a comment on things
at home as abroad. In most ways, the island merely
reduces the way of life in London to bare essentials,
with a change of hierarchies. Questions of marriage,
and of leadership dominate. Ernest's trial run for his
speech in the first act begins: 'Suppose you were all
little fishes at the bottom of the sea...' (CP, 346). He
never completes the sentence, but, in the context of the
play, we must conclude that one fish would take charge
of the others. The words 'nature' and 'natural', which
run throughout the play, mean, in Barrie's terms, the
rule of the strong.

Laurence Irving, whose father was the original
Crichton, believed (surely wrongly) that Barrie did not
see the implications of his own 'deceptively charming
parable'. 'Barrie', Irving says, 'had unwittingly come
nearer to striking at the roots of England's social unease
than G. B. S., for all his Fabian hatchet-work'.[8]

The choice of scene for Barrie's metamorphosis
reflects both his private mythology, and a vogue for
islands in contemporary literature. It also suggests a
revealing parallel with *The Tempest*. Like Prospero,
Crichton finds himself renouncing the power which the
island has given him. The parallel accentuates the
difference. Forgiveness and powers of reconciliation
cannot flourish in the debased world of *The Admirable
Crichton*.

Barrie attempted to repeat the formula of *Crichton*
with a three-act play, *Little Mary*, first performed in the
following year. At the opening Lord Carlton meets a
twelve year old girl, Moira Loney, whose highly
developed maternal instincts have expressed themselves
in fostering four children, all sleeping in boxes around
her. The dialogue between Moira and Carlton contrasts
the innocence of one speaker with the sophistication of
the other. When Moira asks if Lord Rolfe, Carlton's

sixteen year old heir, is 'doing for himself', his father replies:

> Lord Carlton: ...He will never do for himself. (With some feeling) You have a house and grandfather to look after, my child, and four boxes to fill up the time, while he is still at school playing marbles, or the like, and presently he will go to Oxford to play more marbles, or I may send him into the Army to play marbles there.
> Moira (amazed): But won't he tire of marbles?
> Lord Carlton: Oh yes, we tire of them, but we go on playing.
> Moira: But when he gets married?
> Lord Carlton: They will both play. (CP, 430)

Such dialogue foreshadows Shaw's *Heartbreak House* in which disaster is prophesied for a country whose best educated men and women have nothing to do but make romantic love or ride horses. *Heartbreak House*, *The Admirable Crichton* and *Little Mary* proceed upon the same assumption; that idleness is destructive, not only to the individual but to society.

In the second and third acts of *Little Mary*, Moira, relying upon the lifelong research of her Irish grandfather, introduces an effective form of alternative medicine. Execrated by the doctors, she is loved by her patients, who are roused from their indolence to an enjoyable life of useful hard work. Moira finally decides to defy her grandfather's warnings and to reveal the secret:

> Moira: ...Grandpa had a profound conviction that the dear, darling English people suffer from eating too much.
> Cecil: I shouldn't wonder. I'm told the way the poor gorge on Sundays is perfectly sickening.
> Moira: It isn't the poor Grandpa means. He says

here that what the poor do on Sundays the best
people do every day of the week. They have *three
solid meals a day, lunch, dinner, supper*, and that's why
they have to go to Homburg and such like places
once a year, to be washed out and scraped down.
(CP, 483)

These remarks provoke a horrified reaction,
intensified by Moira's admission that the name of her
cure, 'Little Mary' is a euphemism for the
unmentionable word 'stomach'. After the revelation
comes a swift and unsatisfactory ending to the play,
with Carlton proposing marriage to Moira as long as
she promises to protect him from idleness, smoking and
over-indulgence.

In comparison to *Crichton*, *Little Mary* is laborious,
but it ran for two hundred and eight performances. Its
strictures against smoking and pleas for healthy eating
and drinking strike a modern note. (Barrie himself was
a compulsive pipe smoker with an appalling cough).
Bernard Shaw was astonished at the popularity of what
he described as 'a vegetarian pamphlet — a didactic
lark compared to which my most wayward exploits are
conventional, stagey & old fashioned'.[9]

PETER PAN

Peter Pan, the play which immortalised Barrie, opened
at the Duke of York's on 27 December 1904. The first
night audience responded with warmth and enthusiasm
and, within days, families began to arrive, inaugurating
the play's long association with children and with the
Christmas season.

The sources of *Peter Pan* are many, but the plan to
write a children's play can probably be dated to
Christmas 1901, when Barrie saw one of the first works
of its kind, Seymour Hicks' *Bluebell in Fairyland*. Ever

open to new ideas, he decided to write his own. At the outset, the notes for what Barrie calls 'Fairy Play', are traditional: 'Hero might be a poor boy of today with ordinary clothes — unhappy, &c, in Act 1 — taken into Fairydom still in everyday clothes which are strange contrast to clothes worn by the people of fairydom — (a la Hans Xian Andersen)'.[10]

The best known 'fairy play' is Shakespeare's *Midsummer Night's Dream*, frequently performed in the nineteenth century, and directly echoed in Barrie's own *Dear Brutus*. Shakespeare's play was a popular subject for Victorian painters of 'fairy pictures', for whom the evocation of another, dream, world provided an opportunity to introduce psychological and erotic themes by the back door. Barrie's major plays are characterised by their shift from the real to the fantastic and back again, a pattern to which Peter Pan conforms very precisely. Like many of the best 'fairy paintings', it is a dramatic representation of uncertainties and conflicts.

The theme of the boy who could not or would not grow up was in Barrie's mind long before 1901. In a late chapter of *Tommy and Grizel*, Tommy publishes his last book, *The Wandering Child*, 'a reverie about a little boy who was lost. His parents find him in a wood singing joyfully to himself because he thinks he can now be a boy for ever; and he fears that if they catch him they will compel him to grow into a man, so he runs farther from them into the wood and is running still, singing to himself because he is always to be a boy' (TG, 399). In the context of Tommy and Grizel, the implication is clear. Tommy, we are reminded, 'did not really care for children', and, when a child laughs during a reading of this passage, Tommy boxes the boy's ears.

Barrie's own experience of children centred on the Llewelyn Davies boys. In his fine biographical account,

J. M. Barrie and the Lost Boys, Andrew Birkin records the improvised adventures when Barrie both gave and received ideas, writing down the boys' remarks in his notebooks. Birkin concludes that the stories of Peter Pan and of the fairies in Kensington Gardens were intended for younger children, the pirate games for the older ones. As the family grew up, the boys passed from one stage to the other, but incorporation of the two was made for the benefit of the youngest boys.

This helps to explain the mixture of pirate and fairy elements in *Peter Pan*, elements kept separate in the two works which led up to the play. The bloodthirsty pirate games are found in *The Boy Castaways of Black Lake*, an affectionate pastiche of Ballantyne's *Coral Island*. The fairies appear in the Peter Pan chapters of *The Little White Bird*, Barrie's novel of 1902. His narrator, a middle-aged London clubman, watches a young nursery maid from the window, engineers her marriage, and indirectly brings about the birth of her son, David. He tells David of these events, and then fantasises about the boy's earliest origins as a bird in Kensington Gardens. Peter Pan, the subject of one of the narrator's stories, is a boy who flew away from home at a week old, and still lives with the fairies in the Gardens.

The perpetual childhood of Peter Pan echoes romantic theory. For him the 'shades of the prison-house' never close; he is a boy for ever. In *The Little White Bird*, Peter finds a banknote left floating by the poet Shelley. 'Shelley was a young gentleman and as grown-up as he need ever expect to be. He was a poet; and they are never exactly grown-up' (LWB, 135). The last words remind us that, like Sentimental Tommy, Shelley was a disastrous husband. The name Pan, appropriate for the pipe-playing Peter, recalls the admiration felt by Shelley and other nineteenth century poets for the god of freedom and nature worship. In the year of *The Little White Bird*, 1902, E. M. Forster wrote his 'Story of a Panic', in which the spirit of Pan is contrasted with the restrictions of sterile convention.

More striking is an episode to which Barrie also refers in his play. When Peter decides to go back to his mother, he flies in at her open window, finds her asleep, and elects to come back later. When he returns, the window is closed, and another boy in his place. The narrator glosses this with sentiments later explored in *Dear Brutus*, and here evidently addressed by one adult to another: 'we who have made the great mistake, how differently we should all act at the second chance. But... there is no second chance, not for most of us. When we reach the window it is Lock-out Time. The iron bars are up for life' (LWB, 163). The 'prison-house' is closed, not on the 'growing boy', but on the immortal child on the other side.

The Little White Bird is a disconcerting book. The characterisation of the child, David, and of his mother, is full of precise observation, while the Kensington Gardens passages, enclosed within the narrator's storytelling, are apparently presented as sheer fantasy. There are times, however, when it seems that the reader is called upon to believe in this alternative life, a sensation which becomes more pronounced in both the stage directions of the play and in the later novel of *Peter Pan*. What is being implied is that The Never Land and Peter are part of the common experience of very young children. As they grow older, even the memory is lost.

The play, *Peter Pan*, cost Barrie infinite pains. Changes went on through a series of drafts, revisions were made in rehearsal, and major alterations continued for several seasons. Barrie's initial problems resulted from a lack of theatrical precedent. He rejected the traditional children's entertainment, pantomime: 'What children like best is imitation of real boys & girls (not so much *comic* incidents)'.[10] Even his rumbustious favourite, the harlequinade, originally included in the last act, was cut before the play reached the stage.

He had no problems with the scenes of domestic life in Bloomsbury which frame the more exotic Never Land. For these he drew upon his experience as a writer of social comedy. As an early note put it: 'Important character the mother treated from child's point of view — how mother scolds, wheedles, &c — scene in which children's behaviour to her wd tickle children because they recognise the truth of them'.[11]

In the end, Mrs. Darling comes off lightly, while Mr. Darling is presented as a hypocritical ass. The 'head of the household', assumes an unjustified superiority to his wife and children, but his lack of moral fibre is everywhere apparent. Revealing an exaggerated sense of his own importance, Mr. Darling employs inflated forms of speech: 'Am I master in this house or is she?' and 'Much good my wearing myself to the bone trying to be funny' (CP, 513;512). In this dialogue with his younger son, the father adopts a characteristic speech pattern, repeating words provided by the other speaker:

> Michael (coldly): Father, I'm waiting.
> Mr. Darling: It's all very well to say you are waiting; so am I waiting.
> Michael: Father's a cowardy custard.
> Mr. Darling: So are you a cowardy custard. (CP, 511)

In the fifth act, a supposedly contrite and reformed Mr. Darling wallows in shame and misery, enjoying the attention attracted by his abasement in the dog kennel.

Much of the humour of the play lies here, and it is to be enjoyed, if in different ways, by both adults and children. Even the entry of Peter, late in the first act, scarcely changes the style of drama, as he and Wendy exchange information about their circumstances, like children meeting at a party. The magic, which begins with the entry of Peter and Tinker Bell, flying in through the window, only really gets into its stride when Peter teaches all three children to fly.

The machinery by which the characters 'flew' was far more complicated than for any earlier production. It drove the first director, Boucicault, to distraction, but was essential to the structural effect of the play. The middle acts, set on the island, have to be different in kind to the rest of the play, and the mechanical devices, like the crocodile or the mermaids' lagoon are a visible means of achieving this. Charles Frohman's limitless financial support was an important factor, not just a lucky chance.

Language and patterns of dialogue, used with such skill to differentiate characters in Bloomsbury, are again employed with great care on the island. The children from London, like Lewis Carroll's Alice, continue to use the language of normal life, while those around them sound like characters from books. The Indians speak a form of gobbledygook: 'Scalp um, oho, velly quick'; while the pirates go in for archaism and inversion: 'twas', 'oft', 'I have waited long'. Even the lost boys use excessively formal language. 'This is no bird'; 'Oh mournful day!' (CP, 529;527;531)

Hook's melodramatic speech is in keeping with his flamboyant dress: 'Ay, that is the fear that haunts me'; 'Brimstone and gall, what cozening is here?' (CP, 528, 541). He faces his end with a pretentious soliloquoy: 'All mortals envy me, yet better perhaps for Hook to have had less ambition! O fame, fame, thou glittering bauble' (CP, 560). Peter's language is not the bombastic rhetoric of Hook, nor the repetitious inanity of Mr. Darling, but he poses as outrageously as either. 'Put up your swords, boys. This man is mine'; 'Dark and sinister man, have at thee' (CP, 566–7).

With Peter, role playing is so endemic that no-one knows whether he is telling the truth or pretending.

'Pretending' and telling stories are the raison d'être of
any theatrical performance, but, in *Peter Pan*, these
processes are endlessly commented upon, complicating
the differentiation of theatrical 'truth' from what the
characters recognise as fiction.

The Darling children are skilled in pretending before
they leave Bloomsbury. In the opening scene John and
Wendy play mother and father, and, for Wendy at
least, life on the island is a continuation of the game.
She finds herself acting mother once more, sewing and
serving pretend meals to a large family of boys. Peter is
made most uncomfortable at being made to play
'husband', and, in projected revisions, both John and
Michael offer to 'be' father or 'be' Peter. When they
need a doctor, Slightly plays the part. When Peter tells
Wendy to escape from drowning, he knows that the
kite would carry both of them. He must stay on the
rock because 'To die will be an awfully big adventure'
(CP, 545).

Barrie, however, contrives to have it both ways.
While on one level insisting on ideas of playing games,
on another he implies that this is a real world, to which
only children have access. Indians and pirates 'really'
die, the Darling parents have 'really' been waiting a
long time for the return of their family. If the famous
revival of Tinker Bell in the fourth act risks breaking
this spell, the actual effect is not to alienate the
audience, but to involve it directly in life on the stage.
Granville Barker recognised that the 'half-dread of
reality' which could be a weakness in Barrie's other
plays 'is an obvious strength to Peter Pan...the
exciting hovering of the mind between make-believe
and reality'.[12]

The stress on sex differences, as important on the
island as in Bloomsbury, gives a more disturbing side to
the role playing, extensively explored by Freudian
critics. Wendy, Tinker Bell and Tiger Lily are all

frustrated in their desire to arouse some sexual response in Peter. With Tiger Lily's direct attack, Barrie realised that he had gone too far and virtually deleted the episode. Wendy's politer challenge remains within the limits of a parody game of 'grown ups'. 'What are your exact feelings for me, Peter?' she asks, and receives the unpromising reply, 'Those of a devoted son' (CP, 550). The recent Royal Shakespeare production carried out Barrie's original intention of casting a male as Peter. This removed one level of ambiguity, and reinforced what is suggested in the characterisation of Hook and Mr. Darling (often played by the same actor): that no male ever truly 'grows up', and that Peter is not an aberration, but a type of masculinity.

For Wordsworth and Coleridge, children's stories represented an important stage in the development of the imagination. Dickens argues that the discovery of fiction in childhood is a part of becoming a full human being. Children's fiction is very important in *Peter Pan*, where Barrie both draws upon and parodies other writers, Stevenson, Ballantyne and Fenimore Cooper among them. The results, however, are very different from those envisaged by Dickens and the romantics. Instead of growing through discovery, Peter sticks fast in childhood, he does not develop at all. With his bouncy conceit, he is an evocation of the nature of a boy, as Barrie saw it existing through time.

The play demonstrates that children who do grow up are destined to dreary employment and to marriages like the Darlings'. Are we meant to admire Peter's stand against this fate, or to feel sadness for the excluded child, who looks in through the window, but cannot join the family circle? Is Peter the hero of the play, as the title suggests, or is he a negative figure, refusing life? The unresolved tension is the key to the play's perennial fascination. The proposition is an impossible one, but the public, both in and out of the theatre, instinctively recognises its immediacy. Like Hamlet's, Peter Pan's predicament has obtained a currency among those who know nothing of the author or his plays.

Peter has two adversaries, Captain Hook and growing up. His battle with Hook takes the familiar form of the boys' adventure story. Peter is younger, but cleverer, and children in the audience, however afraid of Hook, can have confidence in Peter's supremacy. This is the external story. When Peter duly drives Hook into the mouth of the waiting crocodile, his victory provides the audience with an effective denouement, neatly coinciding with the return home of Wendy and the boys. That these aspects of the island are not timeless, but subject to mortal limits, is insisted upon by the ticking clock inside the crocodile, and by Wendy's awareness that the moment to leave has come.

The other Peter story, that of his refusal of adulthood, is not bounded by time, and as a result spills over the end of the play, causing Barrie acute difficulties in completing the last act. Since the choice involves no tension, the plot cannot resolve itself. In 1908, a new version of the final scene was performed on one occasion only. Wendy appears as a grown woman, and her daughter, Jane, repeating her mother's Act One dialogue with Peter, sets out with him for the Never Land. As re-introduced in the Royal Shakespeare Company production, this scene, with its stress on the eternal nature of Peter, makes a more satisfying ending than the briefer episode with Wendy a year later with which the play usually concludes.

It does not, however, answer the questions. The contention that this is a challenging example of literary openness, must meet, in the sceptic, the response that the dramatist did not know what to do, and so left his play up in the air. Barrie is known to have been influenced by George Macdonald's mystical story for children, *At the Back of the North Wind* (1871), which provides an instructive contrast with *Peter Pan*. Macdonald's story is a Christian allegory. The child hero, Diamond, learns to understand human beings, and teaches others kindness and love, before returning to the land at the back of the wind, which is death. Barrie turns Macdonald's morality upside down. Peter's characteristic attitude to others is a blend of masterfulness, conceit and cruelty. Far from dying in an odour of sanctity, he continues to exist in a world of his own, forgetting both loyal friends and determined foes. He has gained eternal youth, but not by dying in a state of innocence.

The Llewelyn Davies boys were irritated by the introduction of Wendy, a girl, into their story. Barrie, however, like Carroll with Alice, needed a normal figure to stabilize the drama. The development of the play corresponds with Wendy's adventures, not with Peter's, and she provides the clearest structural link between the play's diverse episodes. Unlike Peter and her brothers, Wendy learns from experience. Her discovery that fairies and mermaids can be unpleasantly aggressive is an indication of the play's ambivalence about its fairytale elements. Barrie is certainly not sentimental, even about fairyland.

No infallible method of judging a play intended for children has yet presented itself. Bernard Shaw, who described Peter Pan as the one play of Barrie's which 'bored' him,[13] told August Strindberg that it was 'ostensibly ... a holiday entertainment for children, but really ... a play for grown-up people'.[14] Its financial success was indisputable. Theatre managers hoped to rival it with Graham Robertson's *Pinkie and the Fairies* or Maeterlinck's *The Blue Bird*, but neither achieved the mystique of *Peter Pan*, not its extraordinary blend of disturbing fantasy and parodic romp.

WHAT EVERY WOMAN KNOWS

Alice Sit-By-The-Fire of 1905 was written as a vehicle for
Ellen Terry. She played the part of Alice Grey, who
returns from many years in India to discover that her
children have got used to living without her. The feeble
plot parodies the 'triangular' plays of the Pinero school.
Amy, the Grey's stage-struck daughter, becomes obsessed
with the idea that Alice (like a 'problem play' heroine)
is going to a man's rooms to retrieve her love-letters.
The play traces the processes of comic misunderstanding,
but at too great length.

What Every Woman Knows of 1908 is in a different
class. This is the most enclosed and complete of Barrie's
best plays. The enigmatic title aptly describes its
movement. Maggie, as a woman, 'knows' instinctively.
Her husband, John Shand, only arrives at knowledge
through a course of education, devised by his wife.
Maggie is the controlling figure, and the comedy lies in
her gift for concealing her own machinations. 'Woman
cd do the work better (any woman knows that),'[15] is
Barrie's comment in an early draft.

Barrie takes up a number of serious issues; love,
adultery, political advancement, women's suffrage, and
treats each with ironic detachment. Like a more
insidious Oscar Wilde, he implicitly mocks the work of
his fellow dramatists, while treating his audience to a
classic well-made play.

The first notes indicate the lines on which Barrie's
mind was moving. In 1898, he recalled an idea already
raised in *The Little Minister*, of a woman who pays for a
man's education in return for a promise of marriage.
He wondered whether he could turn it into a play, and
developed a scenario about three bachelor brothers,
terrified of marriage themselves, who pay a poor man
to marry their sister.

This is Thrums love-making with a vengeance, and
in the final play, concepts of romantic love are

exploded. Maggie, her brothers realise, yearns for a grand passion. After trying to pacify her with expensive presents, they find that they have to buy her a man instead. Later, when Shand falls in love with Lady Sybil Lazenby, Maggie, relying on her appraisal of their characters, throws the lovers together. Shand soon finds that sex-appeal, designated as 'charm', doesn't help to write his speeches. Only Maggie, who is without 'charm', can do that.

This was Barrie's last and best treatment of his own 'international situation' of the talented but humbly-born Scot coming south. He satirises the differences between England and Scotland, not only through the action of the play, but also through a series of justly famous direct statements:

> there are few more impressive sights in the world than a Scotsman on the make. (CP, 693)

> A young Scotsman of your ability let loose upon the world with £300, what could he not do? It's almost appalling to think of; especially if he went among the English. (CP, 682)

The joke is so good that the English audience, for whom it is intended, scarcely feels the barb.

The opening act of *What Every Woman Knows* is brilliantly original. 'He knew', says Cynthia Asquith, 'that he'd taken a considerable risk with that long silence when the curtain first rises — the longest in any play — and so was pleased when this succeeded'.[16] The curtain rises on the living-room of newly rich Scottish quarry-owners, the Wylies. James, the younger and weaker of the two sons, is playing draughts with his father. The elder brother, David, enters, preoccupied with his own thoughts and takes off his boots. The silence is punctuated by the ticking of a clock.

When David finally speaks, he startles his father and brother by quoting from Tennyson's *Maud*, before

announcing that they must find 'Love' for their sister.
From the moment of her entry, Maggie dominates the
act. She refuses to leave the room, even when a burglar
is expected, and plays a discreet, but forceful, part in
the negotiation of her own engagement to John Shand.

Shand, who has been climbing in at night to read
the Wylies' books, rises to near lyricism when he fears
that they will turn him out: 'I'll have to stay on here,
collecting the tickets of the illiterate, such as you, when
I might be with Romulus and Remus among the stars'
(CP, 678).

Barrie's wit is at its dryest when the four men decide
to drink on their bargain. David asks Shand if he
drinks:

> David: . . . You're not a totaller, I hope.
> John (guardedly): I'm practically a totaller.
> David: So are we. How do you take it? Is there
> any hot water, Maggie?
> John: If I take it at all, and I haven't made up my
> mind yet, I'll take it cold.
> David: You'll take it hot, James?
> James (also sitting at the table but completely
> befogged): No, I —
> David (decisively): I think you'll take it hot,
> James.
> James (sulking): I'll take it hot.
> David: The kettle, Maggie.
> (James has evidently to take it hot so that they can
> get at the business now on hand while Maggie goes
> kitchenward for the kettle). (CP, 679–80)

The act ends with a double-take. David tells Shand
that Maggie is twenty-five, and much sought after.
Before the bargain is struck, Maggie, in a burst of
honesty, announces that she has no admirers, and is
twenty-six. After Shand has left, her slower-witted
brother, James, comments: 'It was very noble of her to

tell him she's twenty-six. (Muttering as he too wanders away.) But I thought she was twenty-seven' (CP, 685). He puts out the light, and the curtain falls.

In his notes for the play, Barrie questioned whether he should omit the political element. An earlier attempt to bring politics into a revue about Joseph Chamberlain, *Josephine*, had been less than successful. Later notes, however, refer to what may have been a separate play about a Labour member. In *What Every Woman Knows*, John Shand is a radical liberal, who takes up women's rights as his platform. The women's movement was in the air, 1908 being the year in which the suffragette leader, Emmeline Pankhurst, was sent to Holloway Jail. For the interweaving of a projected political reform with an extra-marital entanglement Barrie had an example near at hand. In January 1908, Harley Granville Barker invited him to play a part in a copyright reading of his new play, *Waste*, which had been savaged by the Lord Chamberlain, the official censor. *Waste* deals with the fall from power of an ambitious politician, Henry Trebell, following a brief affair with a married woman. Her death after an abortion brings about his downfall. Trebell's plans to introduce a bill to disestablish the church are juxtaposed to the private events which lead to his suicide.

Barrie was impressed by *Waste*, and *What Every Woman Knows* contains an implicit comment on Trebell's dilemma. The passage in Act Three where the professional politician, Venables, advises Shand how to change his projected speech and accommodate cabinet opinion is a lighter version of the context of power-seeking and opportunism which surrounds Trebell. Shand's political career is also in the melting-pot, but instead of running off with Lady Sybil or shooting himself, he is forced to come to terms with his own inadequacies, and ends the play laughing aloud for the first time.

Granville Barker himself found Barrie's play 'subtly reactionary', and noted that the dramatist could be 'very dangerous'.[17] It is generally assumed that *What Every Woman Knows* is an anti-feminist play, but its effect is rather different. Daring to focus his play on a plain heroine, Barrie draws the audience into direct sympathy with her. Maggie loves John Shand. If she rejects a gentleman's agreement, and insists upon a legal document to bind him to her, she later frees Shand by tearing the document up. Forced, like Julia in Shakespeare's *Two Gentlemen of Verona*, to watch her lover wooing another woman, Maggie rises to new heights of courage and self-reliance.

Two years after *What Every Woman Knows*, Barrie submitted his overtly feminist play, *The Twelve Pound Look*, to the pioneering repertory season at the Duke of York's Theatre. The season opened in February 1910 with John Galsworthy's *Justice*, and Bernard Shaw's *Misalliance*. In the second week, two plays by Barrie were performed on either side of a fragment by Meredith, *The Sentimentalists*. Both Barrie plays recall Ibsen. *Old Friends* (a weak and unsuccessful work) is concerned with inherited alcoholism, and *The Twelve Pound Look* is a lively and skilful account of the subsequent career of a woman who, like Nora in *A Doll's House*, slams the door of her home and sets off to be a typist. The woman, Kate, finds herself working for her ex-husband, Harry. In their dialogue, Harry, undermined by Kate's lack of interest in his material success, tries to find out the name of the lover for whom she left him. Finally, Kate admits that she had no lover, only a need to secure her own freedom. Once she could type well enough to earn twelve pounds she felt able to divorce him.

The dialogue closes with Kate's accusation that Harry has destroyed the spirit of his second wife, but there is a sting in the tail. After Kate has been sent packing, Lady Sims asks her husband about a typewriter:

> Lady Sims (Inconsequentially): Are they very expensive?
> Sir Harry: What?
> Lady Sims: Those machines? (CP, 780)

1908–1917

Between 1908, the year of *What Every Woman Knows*, and 1917, Barrie wrote a great deal, but few of his plays were of any real substance. Ideas were still scribbled into notebooks, but the entries were more infrequent, and, after 1910, fewer were developed and completed.

In 1913, Barrie gave the delighted Frohman a full-length work, *The Adored One*, later *The Legend of Leonora*. This was one of his few really bad plays. Leonora, originally created by Mrs. Patrick Campbell, is on trial for her life, accused of pushing a man out of a moving train. She explains to the court that her victim had refused to close the window when told that her daughter had a cold. So strong is the argument that Leonora is acquitted. Barrie's powerful streak of fantasy had overshot the mark here. He underestimated the audience's resistance to the idea of wilful murder. His immediate response was to rewrite the play, turning the train episode into a dream, but even this major emendation failed to save it. It was revived again in 1917, this time as a one-act play, *Seven Women*.

The two other full-length works performed in this period were both intended to entertain war-time audiences. The musical *Rosy Rapture* (1915), was another disaster, and, if *A Kiss for Cinderella* (1916) was a triumphant success, it is hard to imagine this soft-centred fantasy casting the same spell today. Barrie's Cinderella, Miss Thing, is a girl from London's East

End, who works herself into the ground to support four orphan children, and believes that she will marry Prince Charming. Barrie himself thought the dream ball-scene of the second act was the best he had ever written. Poverty and deprivation underlie the humour, and the play exemplifies a doctrine propounded by him in 1889: 'True humour and pathos can no more exist apart than we can have a penny-piece with only one side'.[18]

Between 1905 and 1918, Barrie wrote a considerable number of one-act plays. Nineteen were produced in the West End, and as many more probably existed in manuscript. Some were performed for the war effort or for dramatists' appeals, and most of these are little more than vehicles for famous actors and actresses, never printed and best forgotten. For the dramatist, the short plays were always a second best, often taken out of his desk to pacify the dogged Charles Frohman. Some, like *Rosalind*, were originally projected in three acts, while others, including *The Will*, are skilfully structured out of three brief scenes, like précis of full length plays. More imaginative than most are two of the wartime plays, *The New Word* and *A Well-Remembered Voice*, which explore the problem of finding a language of feeling so that fathers and sons, normally emotionally restrained, can express their love.

Taken as a whole, Barrie's output of short plays is extraordinarily uneven. The few brilliant hits, like *The Twelve Pound Look* or *The Old Lady Shows Her Medals*, are matched by the resounding misses. A comment in Cynthia Asquith's diary suggests why. On 2 November 1918, she quotes Barrie: 'Not long ago...I wrote — I don't know how many — one-act plays. I was simply slinging them off — I believe I wrote six in one week. But scarcely any of them seemed to be worth keeping. If only...I could exchange this spate for ONE engrossing idea!'[19]

The most startling of Barrie's one-act plays is 'The Fight for Mr. Lapraik' of 1916. The name Lapraik, with its echoes of Stevenson's *Catriona*, is a clue to the play's frightening exploration of the divided mind. The inspiration was a real nightmare in which Barrie's 'degenerate self' tried to push him out of bed and take his place. He ran to his mother (long since dead) for protection, but in vain. Next day, the other self and he had changed roles. Glossing the dream, Barrie said: 'It had really been a gradual process...Do we change? Only in the way we see we have deteriorated (or reverse) when we compare now with 20 years ago'.[20] Barrie considered writing a poem, but eventually produced an unpublished short story about an actress, 'Mrs. Lapraik', and a very frightening play.

By using two actors for the leading role, and exploiting the revolving stage of the Coliseum Theatre, Barrie meant to keep his audience in disturbing suspense. He comes close to developing his own form of expressionism in a search for new ways to present the workings of the mind on stage. 'Mr. Lapraik' was typed, but never performed, but it seems to signal the end of the drought.[21] In the next few years Barrie wrote two of his finest plays, *Dear Brutus* and *Mary Rose*.

NOTES

1. 'Preface' to *The Boy David* (Uniform Edition, 1938), p. X.
2. E. Terriss, *Ellaline Terriss by Herself and with Others* (1928), p. 137.
3. I. Vanbrugh, *To Tell My Story* (1948), p. 67.
4. H. Granville Barker, 'J. M. Barrie as a Dramatist', *The Bookman*, XXXIX, No. 229 (October, 1910), 15.
5. Vanbrugh, p. 68.
6. Beinecke Library, Barrie Mss, A2/15.
7. H. M. Walbrook, *J. M. Barrie and the Theatre* (1922), p. 69.
8. Laurence Irving, *The Precarious Crust* (1971), pp. 64–5.
9. G. B. Shaw, *Letters*, ed. D. H. Laurence (1972), II, 383.
10. Beinecke Library, A2/20.
11. Ditto, A2/23.

12. Granville Barker, p. 14.
13. M. Meisel, *Shaw and the Ninieteenth Century Theater* (Princeton, 1963), p. 326.
14. Shaw, *Letters*, II, 907.
15. Beinecke Library, A2/5.
16. C. Asquith, *Portrait of Barrie* (1954), p. 21.
17. Granville Barker, p. 20.
18. J. M. Barrie, 'Thomas Hardy: The Historian of Wessex', *Contemporary Review* (July 1889), p. 66.
19. Asquith, pp. 23–4.
20. Beinecke Library, A2/35.
21. The play was published in *New Plays Quarterly* (1947).

CHAPTER VIII

DEAR BRUTUS AND MARY ROSE

In February 1917, Barrie told his old friend, A. E. W. Mason, of his anxiety at not being able to find a good subject for a play. Mason suggested that he complete an old idea known as 'The Second Chance'. The play, *Dear Brutus*, was written in a few weeks, and it opened at Wyndhams on 17 October.

Barrie's notes for 'The Second Chance' begin in 1904, with an outline plan which altered very little over the years. The characters were to regret the choices they have made in life. They have their second chance, but at the end return to where they were. Barrie pondered whether the second chance should come in a dream, but decided that the characters, once inside the new life, should have no memory of the old.

The early plans suggest that 'The Second Chance' will be a short play in three scenes, like *The Will* or *Half an Hour*. In turning the scheme into a full-length play, Barrie added depth and quality. A group of characters are gathered together for a house party. On Midsummer Eve they go into an enchanted wood, where each finds his or her wishes fulfilled. At the end of the play, they return to the drawing-room of their host, Lob, and realise that he has been responsible for their adventure.

Dear Brutus and Barrie's next play, *Mary Rose*, have much in common. Both draw upon folk-lore for a plot where human beings are decisively, but not permanently, changed in an enchanted place; Lob's wood in *Dear Brutus*, a Hebridean island in *Mary Rose*.

Neither place is stable. Local tradition has it that Mary
Rose's island was not always there, and Lob's wood
only appears on Midsummer Eve: 'It is never twice in
the same place apparently. It has been seen on different
parts of the Downs and on Moore Common; once it
was close to Radley village and another time about a
mile from the sea' (CP, 1007).

Both plays follow a classic Barrie pattern. They open
with an act in the apparent safety of a well-established
household, and then move to the scene of
metamorphosis. The final act returns to the original
setting and explores the effects of change.

Dear Brutus has a comparatively large cast, but is
tightly concentrated as a demonstration of cause and
effect. Barrie probably never achieved greater dramatic
control than in this relatively short play. The theme of
the second chance is illustrated through several
characters or groups of characters, each succinctly
sketched in the first act. A reader can find background
information, not available to a theatre audience, in the
lengthy stage directions, added after the play's first run
for the Uniform Edition. Most of the 'second chance'
illusions of the characters are, however, clearly
expressed on stage during the first act. Matey, the
pilfering butler, whose theft of three rings begins the
play with a false start, believes that, had he taken a
clerkship in the City, he would now be an honest man.
The philandering John Purdie thinks that his mistake
has been to marry Mabel and so miss the chance of
marrying Joanna Trout. Alice Dearth regrets that she
did not accept her aristocratic suitor, Freddy Finch
Fallowe, in preference to her artist husband, Will
Dearth. Dearth himself believes that the absence of
children has encouraged his alcoholism and despair.
Mr. and Mrs. Coade are the oldest of Lob's guests.
Coade's illusion is that he could have written a great
book, but she, 'the nicest' (CP, 996) of them all, has no
real regrets, and never enters the wood.

Barrie's play is close in theme to Robert Frost's poem, 'The Road Not Taken', which ends 'And that has made all the difference'. Barrie asserts the opposite, that there is no difference, and that 'What really plays the dickens with us is something in ourselves. Something that makes us go on doing the same sort of fool things, however many chances we get' (CP, 1045). The point is put most strongly through the self-deception of Purdie, as he talks to Joanna Trout about his wife, Mabel. The bitter comedy lies in the characters' hypocritical belief in their own sincerity:

> Joanna: I am very fond of Mabel, Jack. I should like to be the best friend she has in the world.
> Purdie: You are, dearest. No woman ever had a better friend.
> Joanna: And yet I don't think she really likes me. I wonder why?
> Purdie (who is the bigger brained of the two): It is just that Mabel doesn't understand. Nothing could make me say a word against my wife —
> Joanna (sternly): I wouldn't listen to you if you did.
> Purdie: I love you all the more, dear, for saying that. But Mabel is a cold nature and she doesn't understand.
> Joanna (thinking never of herself but only of him): She doesn't appreciate your finer qualities. (CP, 1010)

In the wood, Purdie and Mabel talk in the same way about Joanna, whom Purdie now supposes to be his wife. For Purdie, life in the wood is the same as life outside. For others, the change is more advantageous. Lady Caroline is probably happier as a married woman; if Matey is still dishonest, his circumstances are more comfortable. The most likeable of the characters, Will Dearth, would certainly be better off with the daughter whom he finds in the wood, and with whom

E

he seems to recapture earlier joy. Dearth's central position is stressed by the arrangement of the acts. The second leads up to the passage between Dearth and the dream-daughter, Margaret, and in the third, the return of each group of characters reaches a climax as Dearth awakes to the discovery that he is childless.

In the long stage-direction with which the Uniform version begins, Barrie states that the subject of the play is to be the struggle of darkness and light. As the curtain opens, the room is dark, the garden moonlit. The flowers, Lob's accomplices, are, like him, creatures of light, the guests in the house 'dwellers in darkness' (CP, 995). When the women characters enter they switch on the light, so 'that the garden seems to have drawn back a step as if worsted in the first encounter. But it is only waiting' (CP, 996). Lob reverses the effect when he turns out most of the lights before the party go into the 'sombre wood' (CP, 1020).

Inside the wood the world is bathed in moonlight, but at the end of the second act, it fades as the audience gradually loses sight of Margaret in the shadows. The final scene is played out in an obscurity which only brightens when the curtains are opened at the end, to reveal Lob among his flowers in the morning sunshine.

The characters' adventures are associated with this imagery of light and dark, the light of self-knowledge, the dark of illusion. Their passage, like Dante's, takes them from a dark wood towards the light of revelation. When Purdie comes back into the drawing-room, his mind is still 'illumined', and the penultimate direction of the play describes the Dearths 'breasting their way into the light' as they attempt to rebuild their relationship (CP, 1060).

The title of the play comes from Shakespeare's *Julius Caesar*. In the third act of *Dear Brutus*, Purdie, the cleverest of Lob's guests, realises that he is a congenital philanderer, and declares:

Purdie:...I haven't the stuff in me to take warning.
My whole being is corroded. Shakespeare knew what
he was talking about —
      'The fault, dear Brutus, is not in our stars,
      But in ourselves, that we are underlings.' (CP, 1046)

In *Julius Caesar*, the words are spoken by Cassius,
inciting Brutus to be active rather than passive, and to
kill Caesar. Brutus and Cassius carry out the murder,
and the result is not only Caesar's destruction, but their
own. One cannot relate the situation of Brutus and
Cassius precisely to the events of Barrie's play, which is,
in any case, scattered with other Shakespearean
references. The moving wood recalls *Macbeth*. At the
start of Act Two, Lady Caroline and Matey describe
themselves as Rosalind and Orlando, while echoing
Jessica and Lorenzo from *The Merchant of Venice*.
Shakespearean archaisms ('lass', 'lately', 'Philomel')
abound in their endearments (CP, 1022).

A Midsummer Night's Dream provides the most telling
parallel. Entering a wood on Midsummer Night, the
characters temporarily change partners and identities,
before resuming their normal roles, Bottom as a weaver,
Titania as the wife of Oberon. Something of this
pattern of resolution is found in *Dear Brutus* as Joanna
Trout renounces her flirtation with Purdie. The
awakening of Matey and Lady Caroline parallels
another scene in *A Midsummer Night's Dream*, where the
Queen of the Fairies discovers with horror that she has
been 'enamoured of an ass'.

Oberon is the instigator of the changes in *A
Midsummer Night's Dream*, but the actual instrument is
Puck, to whom Barrie gives one of his alternative
names, Lob. Like Puck, Lob is ageless, and is associated
locally with the age of Queen Elizabeth. Like Puck,
Lob has a mischievous, and often malicious, nature.

Throughout the third act, he reflects on his sleeping face his glee at the success of his machinations.

Barrie's is by no means the only twentieth century Puck. Another contemporary example is Kipling's in *Puck of Pook's Hill*. Barrie's creation is far more disturbing, although Will Dearth, who has apparently suffered most from the metamorphosis in the wood, rejects Purdie's assertion that their host is an 'old ruffian'. 'No, I am rather fond of him', replies Dearth, 'our lonely, friendly little host. Lob, I thank thee for that hour' (CP, 1059).

The late romances of Shakespeare are all concerned in some way with the reconciliation of a father and daughter. The sadness of *Dear Brutus* is that the meeting in the wood is to be the only one, not a coming together but a tantalising glimpse. The scene between Dearth and Margaret is almost unbearable, particularly when Margaret expresses relief that she is not a mere shade, but a real flesh and blood young girl. The source for her final desperate plea, not to become a 'might-have-been' is apparently one of Barrie's favourite writers, Charles Lamb. In his essay 'Dream-Children', the childless Lamb writes of an imaginary son and daughter who finally disappear: 'while I stood gazing, both the children gradually grew fainter to my view, receding, and still receding till nothing at last but two mournful features were seen in the uttermost distance'. The essayist senses that they are calling to him: 'We are nothing; less than nothing, and dreams. We are only what might have been, and must wait upon the tedious shores of Lethe millions of ages before we have existence, and a name'. 'Dream-Children' controls its latent grief through the calm of its conclusion: 'I found myself quietly seated in my bachelor arm-chair, where I had fallen asleep'.[1] At the end of Act Two of *Dear Brutus*, by contrast, there is a mounting horror as darkness envelops the young girl:

(... She tries dutifully to count her hundred, but the wood grows dark and soon she is afraid again. She runs from tree to tree calling to her Daddy. We begin to lose her among the shadows).

Margaret (out of the impalpable that is carrying her away): Daddy, come back; I don't want to be a might-have-been. (CP, 1040)

This is Barrie at his most haunted, and one of the few places in his plays where his own dread of vacancy emerges. Dearth's brave words in the final act refer only to himself. Margaret, more tellingly than the unborn son, Timothy, in *The Little White Bird*, remains a disembodied spirit, somehow hovering in the 'impalpable'. Pirandellian explanations that she is a character conjured up by the author and then discarded fail to dissolve the notion that she has been left eternally wandering in a limbo-like wood. If the play can reach unexpected heights in the theatre, it is not because of its neat and tidy plot, but because Barrie does not soften the blow, and allows his dark vision to hold sway. Unhappily, his nerve failed him at the time of the first production, and he reintroduced Margaret, skipping behind her 'parents' in a tableau which preceded the fall of the curtain. By the time of the Uniform edition, however, Barrie recognised that he had falsified the conclusion of his play. Margaret was omitted from the third act, and the final concord between the Dearths becomes a more uncertain, tentative, thing, deprived of unnatural brightness.

From at least 1901, Barrie was fascinated by the idea of the ghost mother who comes back to earth to look for her children, and who, in a darker treatment of the same theme, may kill her grown-up son as a usurper. There are ideas for a play on the subject, together with others for *Dear Brutus*, in a notebook entry of 1904, and, over the years, Barrie speculated further about the return of the dead. In 1919, when at work on *Mary*

F

Rose, he told a friend that his left hand (which writer's cramp had forced him to use) was trying 'to egg me on to making a woman knife her son' (L, 130).

The subject-matter of the play was strange, even for Barrie. Mary Rose, a happily married woman of twenty-four, disappears from a small Hebridean island, and returns twenty-five years later, completely unchanged and unconscious of the time which has passed. Her parents and her husband have aged and 'got over' her loss, while her son, Harry, has run away to Australia. Mary Rose survives as a ghost or spirit, searching through the house for her lost baby. When Harry finally returns as a grown man, she does not recognise him, but his kindness releases her, and at the end of the play she apparently returns to the island.

Between the first manuscript and the production there was a reduction in length of about a third, and a corresponding increase in dramatic clarity. Many of the changes were evidently made in rehearsal and, in its later version, *Mary Rose* is a short play, each act mingling comedy and tension before reaching a strongly developed climax. In the two framing scenes, at the beginning and end of the play, the prodigal son returns to the empty house. Both first and third acts also have a passage in the past with Mary Rose's parents, the Morlands, while the middle act, the climax of the play, takes place on the island where Mary Rose picnics with her husband, Simon Blake, and the highlander, Cameron. At the end of that act, she disappears.

The Uniform edition text, with its extended stage directions, tries to convey the human qualities of the dimly lit opening set. The room is almost bare of furniture, the peeling wallpaper leans forward 'as men have hung in chains', but the light is 'mellow' and there is 'a disturbing smile on the room's face'. The surviving easy chair is 'doddering' like 'some foolish old man', an indirect reference to the heroine's father who once sat in it. The whole room takes on the qualities of his daughter:

> We might play with the disquieting fancy that this room, once warm with love, is still alive but is shrinking from observation, and that with our departure they cunningly set to again at the apparently never-ending search which goes on in some empty old houses. (CP, 1085)

Two figures, the frightened housekeeper, Mrs Otery and the long lost Harry, enter this sinister room. At the opening of *Dear Brutus* the darkness is scattered by the flick of an electric light switch, here it needs a journey of thirty years into the past to transform the set to apparent cosiness and comfort. There is a difficult theatrical moment, both in the first and third acts, when the room suddenly changes by moving forward or backward, and, through this visual juxtaposition, the terrible ravages of time and human loss are made explicit to the audience. While Harry's dream-visions of the past, which provoke these juxtapositions, can be dismissed as mere dramatic devices, they do correspond to his mother's movements from one world to another, and suggest a shared capacity for crossing a barrier of time and space.

Harry's comments on the furniture he knew as a child are made against the bleak background of the opening set, and when, after the time shift, the room is restored, we recognise its ephemeral nature, and await its inevitable disappearance at the end. A part of Harry's role is to state the play's theme by trying to equate memory and actuality: 'I was a little shaver when I was here last, but I mind we called the drawing-room the Big Room; it wasn't a little box like this' (CP, 1086).

Barrie had great difficulty in perfecting the dialogue for the opening scene, and worked over it more

extensively than any other part of his play. He had to
present two comparatively unsympathetic characters,
whose secondary function was to impart pertinent
information to his audience. In 1920, Harry would
have been a recognisable figure, a soldier who had
survived, coarsened by experience. With his rough
speech and masculine manner, he provides the strongest
possible contrast to the elfin Mary Rose and to the
charm invested in her love for her baby son. The
exposition of the drama is achieved through this very
prominent irony, a part of the inherent tragedy which
Barrie found in the relationship of mothers with their
sons.

Barrie was more at ease with the reassuring passage
with the heroine's parents and their friend, the vicar,
which follows. Mary Rose appears, climbing into the
drawing-room from the apple-tree. Introducing a
leading character late in the first act is one of the
dramatist's favourite devices, and he rejected his
original idea of bringing her onto the stage much
earlier, gliding in behind Harry as a ghostly figure in
white. The second half of the first act is not all comedy
and happiness. Mr. Morland's pitiful slowness in
realising that his daughter is no longer a child provokes
bitter-sweet laughter. Like Will Dearth in *Dear Brutus*,
he believes that a daughter's marriage is the worst
thing he has to face, blessedly unaware that he will
soon be deprived of her in a much more devastating
way. Simon's request for her hand is followed by the
well-handled exposition of her twenty-day
disappearance from a Hebridean island as a child of
eleven or twelve. An effective anti-climax follows when
Mary Rose tells Simon that she wants to say something
important. Her words are psychologically revealing, but
they are not what Simon fears: 'I may be wrong, but I
think I'll sometimes love you to kiss me, and sometimes
it will be better not' (CP, 1109). However, as often in

Barrie, a sigh of relief is quickly converted into a new tension when she reveals that she has been planning a honeymoon in the Hebrides.

The second act is the heart of the drama. As in *Dear Brutus*, a character crosses from this world to another with results which mingle tragedy with ironic comedy. The introduction of the poor but educated Scot, Cameron, is a stroke of fine dramatic skill. We can laugh wholeheartedly at the by-play between Cameron and Simon, who finds to his dismay that his employee is far more knowledgeable than himself. When Cameron says that he is reading Euripides, Simon explains 'Latin, Mary Rose!' and is told, with faultless politeness: 'It may be Latin, but these in these parts we know no better than to call it Greek' (CP, 1116). The comedy comes to an abrupt end, however, when Cameron begins to account for the island's reputation, even telling the story of Mary Rose's own brief disappearance. Simon hastens to leave the island: but it is too late.

In the manuscript, Barrie noted down, apparently as a sudden thought: 'Titles The Last Time — Farewell'.[2] The dialogue of the second act explores this theme. Simon tells Mary Rose that one day she will see her baby for the last time: 'I mean only that he can't always be infantile; but the day after you have seen him for the last time as a baby you will see him for the first time as a little gentleman'. Mary Rose says prophetically: 'The loveliest time of all will be when he is a man and takes me on his knee instead of my putting him on mine. Oh, gorgeous! (*With one of her sudden changes*) Don't you think the sad thing is that we seldom know when the last time has come? We could make so much more of it' (CP, 1124). There is an ironic fulfilment in the third act when Mary Rose sits (unknowing) on her son's knee, and repeats these lines without understanding their significance.

The closing stage direction of the second act was extensively re-worked. Simon is absorbed in putting out the fire when the 'call' comes to Mary Rose. In the first manuscript a violent commotion is heard, and Mary Rose rises and walks off-stage, with an 'intent look on her face'.[3] The successive changes to the scene each render Mary Rose's disappearance more ominous and frightening. One plan, developed in rehearsal, was for her to disappear in mid-stage with a metallic clang, another was to be accomplished with mirrors, but these were found not to function in certain areas of the auditorium. In the end the heroine simply walked off stage 'as if drawn by some unseen irresistable force'.[4] Barrie was disinclined to use music, and the producer, Holman Clark, tried unsuccessfully to evolve 'strange unearthly noises'[4] with the orchestra. When Barrie eventually heard the music written for the play by the Haymarket's musical director, Norman O'Neill, he recognised that this was the solution. O'Neill adapted two organ pipes for the 'mysterious rumble'[5] with which the call begins, and the 'wordless singing of the "Island Voices"' was played on a carpenter's saw.[6] The rest of the orchestra was more conventional: strings, woodwind, harp, piano, and three women's voices.

The darkening of Barrie's vision in the development of this passage can be paralleled in later scenes of the play. In the first manuscript the island is revealed as a place of perfect happiness, the Never Land, the home of Peter Pan. Behind a gauze curtain the audience was to see the trees through which Peter and the lost boys make their way underground:

> Peter himself emerges & sits on Joanna's [Mary Rose's] tree-trunk playing his pipes. Joanna arrives (from a boat if this can be suggested) and the two meet. They don't kiss or shake hands — they double up with mirth at being together again on what we now realise to be Peter's island. They

claw at each other like two inordinately gay children. He pulls down her hair & puts leaves in it, so that she looks like Wendy. 'The wood' is mysteriously lit up in the background, and exquisite music comes vaguely from it, including the laughter of unseen children. Peter signs jocularly that all is ready and dances off doubled with mirth and playing his pipes. In a similar ecstasy she dances after him. When they have gone we hear the plop, plop, plop, meaning that the island has got her again.[7]

By originally locating Mary Rose's two absences on Peter's island, and by returning her to it at the end, Barrie relied on a direct theatrical reference. He was wise to change the ending, which an audience unfamiliar with *Peter Pan* would find inexplicable and bizarre. Such a radical change raises other important questions. Did Barrie simply suppress this clue in order to give his play a greater air of mystery: or did he decide that Mary Rose had been somewhere else? The *Peter Pan* ending might seem to reduce the seriousness of *Mary Rose*, but there are other parallels between the Peter Pan story and *Mary Rose*, particularly in the novel, *Peter and Wendy* of 1911, where the mystified Peter finds that Wendy is middle-aged.

As the text developed, Barrie gave the ending a more religious, if not specifically Christian, tone: 'there is in it now no unholy sound. It is a celestial music that is calling for Mary Rose...Harry hears nothing, but he knows that somehow a prayer has been answered' (CP, 1148).

Only the critic of *The Observer* seems to have been sensitive to the ambiguity here:

> Behind the pity of ghosthood lurked a deeper horror. Sir James Barrie appeared to deny it, took pains to show that it had no existence, yet in the

end left it a little vague, as if he dared not be
responsible for anything so dreadful, but was not
going to contradict us if we said that it was there.
What if this were not a ghost, but a still living
woman, left behind, by a past that was past? It
hardly bears thinking of; and yet — [8]

The final act of the first manuscript includes a piece
of dialogue intended to clarify this very ambiguity:

> Mrs. Ems [Otery]: It's an unfortunate young lady.
> Harry: Yes it is. Why is she here?
> Mrs. Ems: Her husband was killed in the war, in
> the naval battle.
> Harry: I know.
> Mrs. Ems: Her father and mother are too frail to
> keep house now. They are living with friends not
> far from here.
> Harry: Yes, I'm going to see them presently. But
> she — ?
> Mrs. Ems: They took her with them — but she
> sometimes slips away and comes back here. There's
> something she's always searching for.
> Harry: Her son?
> Mrs. Ems: So you know! The poor soul, there's
> nothing wrong with her, except that she doesn't
> understand about the passing of time. She thinks
> he is here. [9]

In the later texts, Barrie, as in some of his fiction, cut
out the explanation. He gives no account of what
happened between the off-stage scene in the first part of
the third act where Mary Rose asks her husband about
their son, and her later existence as a spirit haunting
the house and frightening tenants and caretakers. Most
of the early reviewers assumed that she died of shock
after hearing the truth, the most plausible explanation,
but one for which there is no evidence in the play.

Harry is not convinced when Mrs. Otery tells him that his mother is buried in the churchyard.

P. L. Goitein, approaching *Mary Rose* from a psychological standpoint in 1926, believed that it was, like *Dear Brutus*, an expression of Barrie's feelings of barrenness and sterility. For Goitein, Mary Rose is a 'dream child', and Harry, rather inconsistently, undergoes therapeutic analysis by attempting to clarify his relationship with his mother. Even Goitein, however, cannot tie up all the ends: 'Tantalising a symbol as it is, the Island beyond the mist leaves us baffled, even at the end, as to the significance it is intended to convey'.[10]

While autobiographical considerations are inescapable in discussion of *Mary Rose*, there is evidence of external sources, some literary, some anecdotal. After Barrie's death, *The Sunday Times* published a letter from Admiral Mark Kerr in which he recalled a lunchtime conversation with Barrie in 1919 about a twelve year old girl who disappeared for ten days during a family fishing holiday in Norway. The girl herself was unable to give any account of her absence.[11] Norway was the original setting for Barrie's island, but it later moved to Handa, off the coast of Sutherland, and then to a lake in the Outer Hebrides.

The siting of the island in the Hebrides suggests a connection with Celtic mythology, and Barrie himself gives a clue to this in a notebook entry for 1905, 'Hogg's "Queen's Wake" a sort of Rip Van Winkle'.[12] *Mary Rose* has been compared with the 'Kilmeny' section of James Hogg's long poem of 1813. Kilmeny falls asleep in the greenwood and disappears for seven years. After a brief return, she goes away for ever. Hogg is deliberately vague about the nature of the other world. Like Barrie, he steers a careful course between evoking either the Celtic land of Faery or the Christian heaven.

Hogg was drawing on a well-known Celtic legend, reworked by a number of later writers, among them William Allingham in the popular poem 'The Fairies' and Walter Scott in his version of the border ballad 'Thomas the Rhymer'. George Macdonald refers to Kilmeny in his *At the Back of the North Wind* and Macdonald's visionary books suggest another influence on Barrie's treatment of 'other worlds'. Around the turn of the century, an important moment for the collection of Irish and Scottish oral legends, the original story of the young bride or maiden wrapt away by the fairies, re-emerges in the work of a number of writers, among them W. B. Yeats in *The Land of Heart's Desire*, Lady Gregory, Lady Wilde, Edward Martyn and Fiona MacLeod in *The Immortal Hour*.

Elements of *Mary Rose* may derive from tales which Barrie had heard in childhood, the 'misty, eerie Highland stories' which Mary Rose encourages Cameron to tell (CP, 1119). Many Celtic tales maintain an ambivalence between the claims of the real, the everyday world, and the appeal of the enchanted land. In some the husband or lover is assumed to be 'right' to try to 'rescue' the bewitched woman. In others there is an implication that life in the other world will be happier. This ambivalence is present in *Mary Rose*, especially in Barrie's earliest versions; later the island is presented as an evil force drawing the heroine away from her earthly loves.

Both Mary Rose and Cameron speak of the island as though it were an independent being, with human characteristics. Even when Mary Rose has left, it still has a power over her. It is of the island that she is thinking at the time of her engagement:

> Isn't it funny, I had almost forgotten about that island, and then suddenly I saw it quite clearly as I was sitting up there. (Senselessly) Of course it

was the little old woman who pointed it out to me. (CP, 1110)

Throughout the play, Mary Rose is associated with growing things, the rowan on the island, the apple tree which blossoms when she falls in love and is cut down at the time of her wintry return. 'She is just a rare and lovely flower' (CP, 1098), says the stage direction which introduces her, and Barrie's choice of name (he had rejected Joanna, Barbara and Lucy) continues this train of thought. Her mother, however, puts forward a more forbidding parallel with flowers, when she tries to explain the change in her daughter after the first disappearance on the island:

> I have sometimes thought that our girl is curiously young for her age — as if — you know how just a touch of frost may stop the growth of a plant and yet leave it blooming — it has sometimes seemed to me as if a cold finger had once touched my Mary Rose. (CP, 1106)

The 'problem' of *Mary Rose* lies in the dichotomy which was inherent from the start. Although the play undoubtedly 'works' in the theatre, no satisfactory philosophical outcome can be deduced from it. The love of a mother for a son is an adult emotion, and a heroine who does not grow up is a child. Mary Rose is, on the one hand, suspended in girlhood, and on the other is a wife and mother who seems likely to spend eternity searching for her 'baby'. Had she been wrapt away before her marriage, the play would have been closer to the legend, and clearer in import, but Barrie had set himself a harder task. In doing so, he was able to bring the subject of his play home to his audience by giving it a dimension common to human experience. In Granville Barker's perceptive words: 'the real and the unreal are boldly mingled; there is neither evasion of the difficulty nor compromise'.[13]

NOTES

1. Charles Lamb, 'Dream Children', *Works of Charles and Mary Lamb*, ed. E. V. Lucas (1903–5), II, 103.
2. Beinecke Library Ms Vault Shelves Barrie, Mary Rose, 1st Manuscript.
3. 1st Manuscript.
4. W. A. Darlington, *J. M. Barrie* (1938), p. ix.
5. D. Hudson, *Norman O'Neill: A Life of Music* (1945), p. 81.
6. C. Asquith, *Portrait of Barrie* (1954), p. 106.
7. 1st Manuscript.
8. *Observer* (25 April 1920), p. 11.
9. 1st Manuscript.
10. P. L. Goitein, 'A New Approach to an Analysis of Mary Rose', *British Journal of Medical Psychology*, VI, part 2 (1926), 199.
11. *Sunday Times* (25 July 1937).
12. Beinecke Library, Barrie Mss, A2/27.
13. 'Introduction' to *The Boy David* (1938), p. xi.

CHAPTER IX

FAREWELL, MISS JULIE LOGAN

In March 1927, the editor of *The Times*, Geoffrey Dawson, asked Barrie for a piece about Adelphi Terrace. Refusing, Barrie said: 'Just leave it at this, that if I do see anything promising, I'll have a shot at it — as perhaps at something else. It isn't that I'm busy. The fact is I think that I am dead. I only seem to be able to do tom fool things'.[1] By 1930, Barrie had recovered sufficiently to begin work on his memoirs. He reprinted a number of early articles, revised for the occasion, and interspersed them with passages of reminiscence. The volume was published privately under the title *The Greenwood Hat*, and distributed to fifty of Barrie's friends for Christmas.

Work on the book seems to have stimulated an unexpected response to Dawson's suggestion. Early in 1931, Barrie started a new story, completed by 30 June. On 6 July, he told Cynthia Asquith: 'It is terribly "elusive" I fear and perhaps mad, but was I not dogged to go through with it!' (L, 224) Barrie offered the story to *The Times*, and asked that it should appear as a free six page supplement to the Christmas Eve number. He himself accepted no payment.

Coming at a time when Barrie's writing career seemed at an end, *Farewell, Miss Julie Logan* is his one undoubted masterpiece in prose. For this late work, Barrie returned to the Scots setting of his early writing. In 1890 and 1891, he had published a series of sketches about a country manse, where the minister's life is dominated by an inquisitive and intrusive servant girl.

The background of the new story is much the same, but this 'wintry tale' is very different from the discursive and amusing sketches of forty years before.

Farewell, Miss Julie Logan takes the form of a diary, written by a minister of twenty-six, Adam Yestreen, when he is snowed-in during the winter of 186–. Yestreen meets Julie Logan, a beautiful young girl. In reality she is a 'stranger', the ghost of a Jacobite heroine reputed to have succoured the Young Pretender. Her name refers to a 'rocking' or 'logan' stone, popularly associated with the supernatural. According to local legend, the Jacobite girl was said to have leapt onto a logan stone while searching for game to feed Prince Charlie.

By telling the story through the words of Adam Yestreen, Barrie is able, as in his plays, to project an individual character without the intervention of a narrating voice. The development of the later plays, through a series of evolving texts, had taught him economy. *Julie Logan* is not a compressed work, but, in dealing with a single theme, it has real virtues of control and organisation. The diary form gives a sense of immediacy, and limits the operation of hind-sight to Yestreen's summing-up in the Epilogue, supposedly written twenty-five years later.

Yestreen's diary reveals how the young minister's struggles after spiritual perfection are constantly undermined from within. Like Gavin Dishart in *The Little Minister*, Yestreen is an innately sensual man whose emotion is unnaturally blocked by the outward demands of his calling. Where the improbable Babbie is conjured up to resolve these tensions in the early novel, here we remain within the mind of Yestreen himself. The story never becomes tortured, or depressing, but it does probe deeply into the fantasies of isolation and repression.

When *Julie Logan* was published in book form in

1932, Barrie took the opportunity to make certain emendations. Early in the story, he added a passage where Yestreen speaks of his response to the trees and shrubs of the manse garden:

> My predecessor, Mr. Carluke, tore down the jargonelle tree, which used to cling to my gable-end, because he considered that, when in flourish (or as the English say, in blossom, a word with no gallantry intilt), it gave the manse the appearance of a light woman. (MJL, 4)

This not only illustrates Yestreen's love of beauty, but also his use of dialect. There are few dialect words in the *Times* version, but, for the book, many English terms were replaced by Scots ones, 'speel' for 'climb'; 'hallan' for 'passage'; 'half nine on the clock' for 'nine o'clock'; 'stramash' for 'distress' (MJL, 23, 35, 37, 47). The changes in Yestreen's vocabulary suggest greater humanity and individuality, and set him further apart from the English visitors, who play with Scots terms in much the same spirit as they wear the tartan. As Yestreen says, they 'have a happy knack of skimming life that has a sort of attraction for deeper but undoubtedly slower natures' (MJL, 12).

Yestreen's private comments on the English reveal the unflattering awareness of the perceptive outsider. When he is asked to take an attractive lady to dinner, the most popular man is placed on 'the other side of her to make up for me' (MJL, 14). When the 'popular man' asks Yestreen to agree that the lady is very pretty, 'all I could reply was that I had not given the subject sufficient consideration to be able to make a definite statement about it' (MJL, 15).

The sharp satire on the English in Scotland introduces Yestreen's diary. It is they who have challenged him to describe his experiences during the winter months, and he accepts with an ill-founded confidence, believing that local stories of 'strangers' are 'superstitious havers, bred of folk who are used to the travail of out of doors, and take ill with having to squat by the saut-bucket' (MJL, 2).

Yestreen's account of the locked glen is in some ways a rewriting of the fine opening section of *Auld Licht Idylls*, 'The School House'. There too, Barrie describes the freezing hens brought into the house, the black burn cutting through the white snow, but a close reading shows a marked difference in emphasis. The ridge 'struggling ineffectually to cast off his shroud' (ALI, 2) of *Auld Licht Idylls*, becomes, in a stronger and more threatening image, 'White hillocks of the shape of eggs' which 'have arisen here and there, and are dangerous too, for they wobble as though some great beast beneath were trying to turn round' (MJL, 32–3).

The early 'School House' passage is largely descriptive and consoling. The narrator manages to rescue a freezing bird, and drags a water-hen from a weasel. In *Julie Logan*, the imprisoning snow has a more profound significance. Snow becomes the outward symbol of Yestreen's isolation from warmth and affection. We are constantly reminded, through the deceptive simplicity of his narrative, that the outer and inner man are at odds, as are the outer and inner statements of the diary entries. Yestreen is not without insight into his own state of mind. He knows, for example, that on his arrival in the glen he walked 'with affected humility' (MJL, 3), conscious of being stared at from every window along the route. With touching dignity, he acknowledges his own immaturity. He looks 'maybe younger than is seemly in my sacred calling, being clean-shaven without any need to use an implement' (MJL, 3).

Yestreen continually reveals his suppressed response to beauty. He loves his garden and his study. He alone likes the ancient yellow-tinted glass in the window at the Grand House. Most telling of all are his references to his violin, which distracted him as an undergraduate and which he fears he should not have brought to the glen: 'I have never once performed on the instrument here, though I may have taken it out of its case nows and nans to fondle the strings' (MJL, 3).

Almost in solitary confinement, cut off from his neighbours by snow, Yestreen begins to hear his fiddle playing to itself. His reproving commentary on his apparent hallucination is expressed in sensible statements which gradually dissolve away as his emotion metamorphoses the violin into a sensuous human being:

> Of course there was nobody. I had come back with the tune in my ears, or it was caused by some vibration in the air. I found my fiddle in the locked press just as I had left it, except that it must have been leaning against the door, for it fell into my arms as I opened the press, and I had the queer notion that it clung to me. I could not compose myself till I had gone through my manse with the candle, and even after that I let the instrument sleep with me. (MJL, 35–6)

Yestreen's response is to decide that 'it might be hard on a fiddle never to be let do the one thing it can do' (MJL, 36), an indirect reflection on what is happening to himself. So he lends the violin to the local postman, with the proviso, often disobeyed, that it shall not be used to play Jacobite lilts. The postman yields himself to the wayward, feminine, qualities of the violin: '"She likes that kind best, and she is ill to control once she's off"' (MJL, 36). Even Yestreen cannot resist the forbidden tunes: 'It is pretty to hear him in the gloaming, letting the songs loose like pigeons' (MJL, 36–7).

As the snow locks him in, Yestreen's only contact

with the outside world is waiting for the old lady at the Grand House to let up her blind twice every evening, and then responding three times with his own.[2] The snow-bound glen is like the night 'waiting, as it must have done once, for the first day. It is the stillness that is so terrible. If only something would crack the stillness' (MJL, 38).

Yestreen's hold on reality gradually evaporates. He thinks that he has written up his diary, but finds only a few broken lines, with 'God help me' written 'as if I were a bird caught in a trap' (MJL, 37). The violin can release songs like pigeons, but, in a reversal of the image, Yestreen is the caged bird.

Local gossip has it that one of Yestreen's distant predecessors, Mr. H., who also kept a diary during the snowy weather, was locked in a desperate struggle against a 'spectrum' with a 'wicked desire to drive the lawful possessor out of the house and take his place' (MJL, 29). Mr. H., like Mr. Lapraik in Barrie's one-act play, was driven out of the house, while the incubus took possession. Doctor John, talking to Yestreen of Julie Logan, hazards a guess that the enchanting young girl is a manifestation of Mr. H's 'spectrum', and that she has appeared in other forms at other times. One of her appearances is in a remote cottage where a woman is about to give birth. Here the 'stranger' brings warmth and close physical contact. After relighting the fire, and helping to deliver the baby, she strips naked and lies next to the mother to act as a hot-water bottle.

In revision, Barrie played down Julie Logan's 'spectrum' side, and put more stress on her romantic, Jacobite, appeal. As a low-church minister, Yestreen officially frowns upon Catholic legends. Half a highlander himself, however, he has to admit privately the attraction of the forbidden.

In the chapter called 'The End of a Song', Yestreen, searching for Julie Logan on New Year's Eve, sits down on the bank of the loch by the Grand House. In the distance, he hears what he calls 'the most reprehensible but the loveliest of all the Jacobite cries, "Will you no come back again?"' (MJL, 76). When the music fades there is complete silence, and, as he looks into the water, Yestreen sees reflected there a scene taking place in the ballroom. His statements are positive, 'I saw', 'I could see', he repeats several times. The indefinite statements, so characteristic of Barrie's prose, relate here, not to doubts about what Yestreen 'sees', but to his uncertainty about the meaning of the vision: 'I could see the trews and an occasional flashing silver button or a gleam of steel; but near all colour had been washed out of them, as if they had been ower long among the caves and the eagles' (MJL, 77).

Encouraged by the silence, Yestreen tries to see directly into the hall, but when he moves, the figures in the reflection become aware of his presence. They are distracted from him by the arrival of Julie Logan, her clothes in tatters, searching for food for the hidden Pretender. Moving out of the mirrored world of the hall, she comes down the steps to the minister, and they eat together in a sheltered corner. The end of the love scene comes when Yestreen, responding to a playful challenge, carries the girl into the middle of the burn. There she tells him that she is a Catholic, and, overcome by the shock, he drops her into the water. Yestreen falls into a nervous collapse, and is ill for weeks, but, when he recovers, the enchantment is over.

By setting his story in the 1860s, the decade of his own birth, Barrie again chose a period when rigid and restricted religious beliefs provided a foil for the aesthetic and the passionate. The choice of the minister's names is significant. Adam Yestreen dislikes his Christian name, 'with its unfortunate associations' (MJL, 2); and his surname, meaning 'yesterday evening', points back to the more immediate past.

Another level of time is introduced by the references to the Jacobite rising. In Stevenson's *Kidnapped*, a book which Barrie knew intimately, the lowland whig, David Balfour, finds himself both attracted and repelled by the highlander, Alan Breck Stewart. Here the half-highlander Yestreen is unable to resist the attractions of the Jacobite and Catholic Julie Logan.

The Epilogue, set twenty-five years later, allows Yestreen to reconsider events. He has moved away from danger, settled in an industrial town and married there. But for all his reiterations that she never existed, he has never forgotten Julie Logan, and the concluding paragraph speculates that, after his death, his younger self will escape into the glen.

Published on Christmas Eve, *Julie Logan* is a traditional winter's tale and ghost story. 1931 is the year in which M. R. James's ghost stories were first published in one volume, and the comparison is instructive. Barrie's supernatural tale offers us a seductive rather than a terrifying visitation. Yestreen has gained rather than lost through his brief release from repression. Because the protagonist is essentially good, the effect of the haunting has been benign.

NOTES

1. Bodleian Library, Dawson Papers, f. 98.
2. Barrie seems to have borrowed this idea from Hardy's *Two on a Tower*, and the same author's 'The Distracted Preacher' may have suggested the character of the young clergyman.

CHAPTER X

THE BOY DAVID

Sixteen years separated the first production of the *The Boy David* from that of *Mary Rose*. Now in his seventies, Barrie resisted the temptation to relive old glories, and struck off across new territories. A career in the theatre which opened with a disastrous historical play, *Richard Savage*, closed with a Biblical drama. Between the two, Barrie had ventured no further than the Napoleonic era for his subject-matter. Neither the Jacobite rebellion nor the story of Mary Queen of Scots ever inspired the Scottish drama of which he intermittently dreamed. Instead, at the request of the actress, Elizabeth Bergner, he turned to the Old Testament story of King David.

A new tradition of historical drama emerged in the 1920s and 1930s. The pioneering work was Shaw's *Saint Joan* of 1924, a play which Barrie greatly admired, and in which Elizabeth Bergner had starred. Through a powerful historical figure, Shaw presents a commentary on contemporary and historical issues. In their very different ways, Bertolt Brecht and T. S. Eliot were among the dramatists who followed his example.

Barrie's research work on Jewish tradition did not lead him to proclaim political or religious truths in his play, although, given its date, he might have done. An assertion of nationality was clearly in the exiled actress's mind when she chose the subject. Barrie's interest lies in the clash of the generations. David, like Shaw's Joan, is a representative figure of youth and power, part of a force destined to sweep away darkness and corruption. Both authors use a well-known story which leads towards an inevitable end. Both decided to quote certain passages from original sources. Barrie's David speaks the opening verses of the twenty-third psalm, and the lamentation over Saul and Jonathan. Unlike Shaw, Barrie makes no startling use of anachronistic dialogue. His characters speak in a heightened style, marked by the prose rhythms and cadences of the Authorized Version.

The writing of *The Boy David* followed a familiar Barrie pattern. He began enthusiastically on the first act, set in the home of Jesse in Bethlehem. David, the youngest son, is despised by his brothers, but loved by his mother. When he says that he has killed a lion, and a bear, no-one believes him. The coming of Samuel, searching for the chosen king among the sons of Jesse, proceeds in the manner of a fairy-tale. David, like a tentative Cinderella, is the chosen one. Barrie departs from the First Book of Samuel in insisting upon Jesse's absence during this scene. When he returns, the father finds that David has eaten his supper. His wrath is deflected, however, by his belief that the boy is in some way possessed. The act ends with David's announcement that he is called to kill Goliath.

Barrie wrote the first act swiftly enough, but then became anxious and uncertain about how to continue. The killing of Goliath was a major obstacle, and scenes were written, rewritten and rearranged as he tried to find a way round. The confidence and completeness of the first act gives way to the more uncertain and uncomfortable second act, laid out in three scenes. Barrie's intention was to run the relationship of Saul and David on parallel lines, and the dramatic tension comes from this relationship, which mingles love, hate and fear. Saul is to some extent the father; loving David, but fearing usurpation by him. Like David's actual father, he falls under the spell of the boy's personality. Barrie originally intended to call the play

'The Two Farmers' or 'The Two Shepherds', and the scene where David and Saul, meeting for the first time, talk of their flocks of sheep, is the finest piece of writing in the play.

By comparison, the crowd scenes seem disastrously stilted. Augustus John's sets for the first production proved theatrically hopeless, but, even without them, it is easy to see why Barrie found the Goliath episode such a problem. At first, he hoped to bring Goliath onto the stage. Then a dummy was tried, but in the end the Philistine giant was reduced to off-stage voice.

Barrie's play is a prologue to the story of King David. Having killed Goliath, David returns to his home and family. Saul continues to reign. The author, however, decided that this was not enough, and incorporated a series of dream visions of the future into the final act. These represent some of the major episodes of David's relationship with Saul, leading up to the death of Saul and Jonathan. David wakes, and the play closes with him as a boy once more, talking with Jonathan.

The visions were a serious problem on stage. The director, Komisarjevsky, failed to unify the third act effectively. There were long pauses while the scenes were changed, often involving the fall of the curtain, and Barrie protested that the status of the visions as dreams was undermined by the lighting, which failed to pick out the sleeping family clearly. Elizabeth Bergner herself, with good reason, felt that an adult man should have played the fully-grown David of the future.

Barrie's venture into the timeless world of dream again suggests the influence of expressionism, or perhaps of the epilogue to *Saint Joan*. *Macbeth* is, however, a more potent source for Barrie's doomed Saul. Like Macbeth with the weird sisters, Saul summons the Witch of Endor only to receive a grim announcement of death and disaster.

Looking back on the play's comparative failure, Barrie said that he had not found the means to express himself. Illness limited his attendance at rehearsals, and, when he finally saw the production, it was too late to make his usual alterations and amendments. Elizabeth Bergner failed to carry off the part of David, a role which surely needs a boy actor. If the play were to be revived, it would be for the tormented and divided figure of Saul. The stage directions tell us that Barrie had Browning's poem and Rembrandt's painting in his mind as he wrote the play. Both works bring out the inherent tragedy in the relationship of David and Saul. Barrie too was acutely aware of this, but seems to have made David too charming to bear the weight of his role. In the end *The Boy David* fell between two stools.

CHAPTER XI

BARRIE AND THE CRITICS

In his lifetime, Barrie had few outright critical successes. The only works to be greeted with almost universal warmth were the early Scottish fictions, *The Admirable Crichton*, *Peter Pan* and *Dear Brutus*, but even here dissenting voices were raised. The challenging *Tommy* novels provoked strong criticism, levelled at their unconventional construction and apparent obscurity. Even a popular play like *Mary Rose*, written when the author was generally admired and esteemed, prompted a mixed response. The writers in *The Saturday Review* and *The Evening Standard* were openly hostile, finding a 'dreadful facility' and an unhappy blend of the 'supernatural' and 'suburban'[1]; conversely, H. G. Hibbert in *The Sunday Times* felt the 'sense of the spiritual' to be 'inevitable, and gripping'.[2] On the whole, the critics were polite if superficial; 'Barrie-ish' and 'Barrie-esque' being familiar soubriquets.[3]

Among Barrie's near contemporaries, Harley Granville Barker was the most discerning and intelligent commentator on his work, although he failed to recognise the excellence of *The Admirable Crichton*. Max Beerbohm, another incisive critic, was nearer the mark. Reviewing *Crichton*, he wrote: 'Mr. Barrie has always been able to amuse us. But this is the first occasion on which he has succeeded in making us also to think'. Barker disliked *Peter Pan*, without, he confessed, having seen it. Beerbohm called it 'the best thing he has done — the thing most directly from within himself', but qualified this with the equivocal statement that Barrie was not a genius, but 'a child who, by some divine grace, can express through an artistic medium the childishness that is in him'.[4]

Bernard Shaw consistently referred to Barrie as a popular writer, even while crediting him with bringing the London theatre out of the Nineteenth Century. 'Mr. Barrie is a born storyteller; and he sees no further than his stories', Shaw wrote in his review of *The Little Minister*, 'The Little Minister is a much happier play than The Tempest'.[5] Barrie always interpreted this as a statement that Shaw thought his plays as bad as Shakespeare's.

The cool reception of *The Boy David* opened the way for a flood of hostile criticism following Barrie's death. The main target of attack was the fiction rather than the plays. Barrie's sense that theatrical dialogue was an effective mask for his personality is shared by many of those who most dislike him.

Barrie's enemies approached on three fronts. On the first score, he was seen as a Scotsman who sold out, making fun of his countrymen for the amusement of Southern readers, and tacitly supporting a conspiracy intended to blunt Scottish radicalism. This school of thought was clearly defined in 1951 with the publication of *Barrie and the Kailyard School* by George Blake. Acknowledging Barrie's superiority to the so-called Kailyard writers, S. R. Crockett and Rev. John Watson (Ian Maclaren), Blake still finds Barrie's early work deeply distasteful.

The second attack can be loosely described as Freudian or psychological. The literary implications were succinctly and intelligently expressed by David Daiches in a radio broadcast of 1960. Daiches condemns Barrie as a talented writer whose own psychology set him outside the normal range of human emotion. Barrie's reaction was to indulge in what Daiches describes as cruel sentimentality. Jacqueline

Rose probes some of the same issues in her study of *Peter Pan*, but her real interest is less in Barrie, than in the general question raised by her sub-title, *The Impossibility of Children's Fiction*.

The third charge against Barrie includes elements of the first two, but can be broadly characterised as stylistic. This focusses on Barrie's sentimentality and on his capacity to stir up emotion for its own sake. *Sir James Barrie* by H. M. Geduld, published in New York in 1971, is a largely hostile account of Barrie's writing in both prose and drama which proceeds upon these assumptions.

None of these criticisms is without foundation, but none tells the whole story. A reaction was already beginning in 1954, with Roger Lancelyn Green's careful study, *Fifty Years of Peter Pan*. Six years later, the same author published a brief monograph in a series on children's writers, again basing his case for Barrie centrally upon *Peter Pan*.

A number of more recent writers have approached Barrie with a conscious effort to break through prejudices and preconceptions. Eric Anderson and Emma Letley have both argued the case for *Sentimental Tommy* as an outstanding novel of childhood. Lynette Hunter sees the Tommy novels as an important stage in Barrie's rejection of fantasy. A new-found maturity, Hunter believes, freed him to write his best drama. For her, *Peter Pan* represents Barrie's repudiation of an inhuman fantasy world. Thomas Knowles takes up the difficult task of reinvestigating the Kailyard, and produces a reasoned and thoughtful account of the early fiction. He scrupulously avoids exaggeration and emotion.

Barrie founded no school of drama. A. A. Milne was sometimes described as a disciple, and Maurice Maeterlinck once declared that *Peter Pan* was the grand-father of *The Blue Bird*, but little else can be ascribed to Barrie's influence. The well made play was already on the way out when Barrie died, and he was regarded as hopelessly out of date in the 1950s and 1960s. The production of *Mary Rose* at the Shaw Theatre in 1972, however, aroused an enthusiastic critical response. This, with other recent productions, makes it clear that Barrie can still capture an audience. Reprints of the *Tommy* novels and of *Farewell, Miss Julie Logan* would be the next step forward.

NOTES

1. *Saturday Review* (8 May 1920), p. 430 and *Evening Standard* (23 April 1920), p. 6.
2. *Sunday Times* (25 April 1920), p. 8.
3. *Pall Mall Gazette*, p. 4; *Times*, p. 14 (both 23 April 1920).
4. G. Rowell (ed.), *Victorian Dramatic Criticism* (1971), pp. 276, 278 and 279.
5. G. B. Shaw, *Our Theatre in the Nineties* (1932), III, 244.

SELECT BIBLIOGRAPHY

Collections
The Thistle Edition. New York, 1896–1902.
The Kirriemuir Edition. 1913–22.
The Uniform Edition of the Works. 1913–22.
The Uniform Edition of the Plays. 1918–38.
Plays, ed. A. E. Wilson. 1942. (Definitive Edition).

Bibliography
H. Garland. *A Bibliography of the Writings Of Barrie*.
  1928
B. D. Cutler. *Barrie: A Bibliography*. 1931.
W. M. Jones. *Writings on Sir J. M. Barrie*, unpublished
  dissertation for the London University Diploma in
  Librarianship. 1964.

Biography
D. Mackail. *The Story of JMB*. 1941.
C. Asquith. *Portrait of Barrie*. 1954.
J. Dunbar. *J. M. Barrie*. 1970.
A. Birkin. *J. M. Barrie and the Lost Boys*. 1979.

Stage History
I. F. Marcosson and D. Frohman. *Charles Frohman*.
  1916. With an appreciation by J. M. Barrie.
I. Vanbrugh. *To Tell My Story*. 1948.
J. C. Trewin. *The Theatre Since 1900*. 1951.
A. Nicol. *A History of English Drama*, Vol. V: 1850–
  1900. 1959.
A. Nicol *English Drama: 1900–1930*. 1973.

Criticism

H. Granville Barker. 'J. M. Barrie as Dramatist', *The Bookman*, XXXIX, No. 229 (London, Oct. 1910), pp. 13–21.

H. Granville Barker. 'Introduction' to *The Boy David* by J. M. Barrie, 1938.

H. M. Walbrook. *J. M. Barrie and the Theatre.* 1922.

T. Moult. *Barrie.* 1928.

J. A. Hammerton. *Barrie: The Story of a Genius.* 1929.

J. A. Roy. *J. M. Barrie.* 1937.

W. A. Darlington. *Barrie.* 1938.

G. Blake. *Barrie and the Kailyard School.* 1951.

R. L. Green. *Fifty Years of Peter Pan.* 1954.

R. L. Green. *J. M. Barrie.* 1960.

D. Daiches. 'The Sexless Sentimentalist', *The Listener*, LXIII (12 May 1960), pp. 841–3.

A. Wright. *J. M. Barrie.* 1976.

L. Hunter. 'J. M. Barrie: The Rejection of Fantasy', *Scottish Literary Journal*, V, No. 1 (May 1978), pp. 39–52.

E. Anderson. 'The Kailyard Revisited', in *Nineteenth Century Scottish Fiction*, ed. I. Campbell. 1979.

A. E. C. Letley. *Literary Uses of Scots Dialects in Certain Nineteenth Century Novelists, from John Galt to George Douglas Brown.* Unpublished London University Ph.D. thesis. April 1983.

J. Rose. *The Case of Peter Pan.* 1984.

T. D. Knowles. *Ideology, Art and Commerce. Aspects of Literary Sociology in the Late Victorian Scottish Kailyard.* Göteborg. 1983.